Famous Past Lives

Famous Past Lives

Steve Burgess

BOOKS

Winchester, UK
Washington, USA

First published by O-Books, 2011
O-Books is an imprint of John Hunt Publishing Ltd., Laurel House, Station Approach,
Alresford, Hants, SO24 9JH, UK
office1@o-books.net
www.o-books.com

For distributor details and how to order please visit the 'Ordering' section on our website.

ISBN: 978 1 84694 494 9

A CIP catalogue record for this book is available from the British Library.

Design: Tom Davies

Printed in the UK by CPI Antony Rowe
Printed in the USA by Offset Paperback Mfrs, Inc

We operate a distinctive and ethical publishing philosophy in all
areas of our business, from our global network of authors to
production and worldwide distribution.

CONTENTS

ACKNOWLEDGEMENTS

Writing this book has been something of a labour of love, in that I've been writing about something which I am a passionate advocate for, namely the importance of Past Life Regression. I would like to particularly thank those clients whose stories appear in the book, not only for trusting me with their therapy in the first place but also for their support when they knew I was writing the book. Each one of them is a good, honest person who was just as surprised as I was when they experienced their famous past life.

I would also like to thank my good friend and excellent therapist Michelle Hardwick for proof-reading the manuscript and for making suggestions of improvements to my inelegant prose, and my dad who overcame his scepticism and who enjoyed the book whilst he went looking for typos. Words of gratitude too to my actress friend Michelle Holmes, who kept inspiring me when I lost impetus.

Lastly, and perhaps most importantly, to all of my clients over the years, from whom I have learned so much and without whom I would not be the therapist I am today.

'May all beings be happy
May all beings be free from suffering
May all beings be at peace
May all beings have balanced minds, free from hatred and attachment'

OM MANI PADME HUM

Foreword

I first met Steve Burgess at a hypnotherapy conference, where he was doing a talk on Past Life Regression. I sat and watched Steve give a very elegant, eloquent, humorous and most importantly, passionate history of his findings in PLR and how he used it to great effect with so many clients. I was 'trance-fixed' as I listened and laughed at his stories. I was however, not convinced. Steve and I talked socially later and I think he sensed my cynicism as he suggested I attend one of his courses to see for myself. I said I would 'think about it' and I did think about it, for about five years. By this time I had created for myself a thriving Harley Street practice and was also having great success as an international trainer even sharing the stage on occasion with Paul McKenna (excuse me whilst I pick up that name I just dropped). I had over the years been fortunate enough to train with the best, the elite, in therapeutic intervention. I had been on a couple of Steve's seminars in the past and really enjoyed his style and delivery.

One uncharted area for me though was PLR, and I thought, 'well you can't really comment until you train and qualify in it', and thus I booked myself on to Steve's next course. I went in blind, having minimal knowledge and without pre reading any subject matter and never having tried it myself in practice. So there I was sitting in a PLR with a group of others, many in the main, great believers in PLR, alien abduction, angels and whatever else lay in the extremes of the esoteric realm. I was in a room full of strangers, and took comfort in the fact that there were many stranger than I. Steve went around the group asking us to introduce ourselves and say why we were there. I gave my name and when prompted as to why I was there, recall answering with a smile *"well you only live once"*. This elicited a couple of giggles, including from Steve, and a number of scowls all aimed in the direction of this particular heretic.

I took full part in the training, listening to what Steve told us and did the exercises diligently with those who got the short straw and were paired with me.

On one particular exercise, a strange thing happened. I had an experience, which I fully recall in great detail to this day. I went through the process and seemed to regress to 'something'. It was 1140 (the year not the time) and my name was Adam. I was in Provence in France and lived as a woodsman, living off the land and alone. I remember eating a meal from a wooden platter and going to my bed with a strange sensation that I would not awaken to see another morning. I did this peacefully and without fear and experienced in trance what I guess was the dying process. I recall it was peaceful and calm and I then, and have since found great comfort in this experience. I exited the trance and instantly began to analyse or (anal-lies) the experience and began to wonder if it was truly a past life or just a metaphor. I truly do not know and truly do not care. It was an experience and I am glad I had it. I have since done a number of PLR sessions in Harley Street with clients, quite a few who are celebrities and are just 'curious'.

In the main nothing has happened except the client has had a nice relaxing hypnotic trance, however, on occasion I have witnessed some quite bizarre reactions into past life, sometimes guided and sometimes spontaneous and a few times the client has experienced what may be determined as a past life trauma that has somehow carried over and is creating a disturbance in their current life. Once the past life issue has been cleared, however, the present day issue also seems to clear up. Once again I do not know if it is a true PLR or a very powerful metaphor, what is important though is a process has been gone through and the client feels better. I have Steve to thank for enabling me to have this particular tool in my box and teaching me well in how to use it to best effect. Over time I have become much more open-minded and am now doing some 'out there' things myself. I am also an author and fully understand how difficult it is to write a book, especially one that will engage the reader throughout. To this end Steve has done an outstanding job with this work. I have had the honour to pre-view this work and was at minimum 'flattered' when Steve asked me to write his foreword. I have enjoyed doing so and only hope I do the rest of this book justice.

Kevin Laye Hypnotherapist and Author of *'Positive Shrinking'*
www.kevinlaye.co.uk

Ps. I would like to leave you with a final thought, especially to those cynics of whom I both once was, and in some ways still am. If you need tangible proof, you know something you can touch or see or wheel about in a wheelbarrow, then let me ask you this. Do you love someone? If you answer yes, then I further ask you to prove it. What colour is it? What shape is it? How do you measure it? Lbs-inches-nanometers, joules, %'s or perhaps $'s?

Tell you what; just wheel it in, in front of me in a wheelbarrow to prove it exists. Then and only then will I believe you, okay?

"The mind is like a parachute, it works best when it is open"

Chapter 1

Trust me, I'm a Therapist

What follows may appear too fantastic to be true. To be honest, I'm still coming to terms with it all myself. You see, for over 10 years as a hypnotherapist in private practice I conducted many thousands of Past Life Regression sessions with my clients, usually helping them to eradicate problems in their present lives by going back to the root causes of the issues which were caused by traumatic events in previous lifetimes.

My viewpoint during those 10 years was that anyone who claimed to have been someone famous in a past life was likely to be making it up, simply being egotistical because they wanted to feel important or draw attention to themselves. Also, the myth about Past Life Regression (fondly propounded by the media) is that everyone undergoing regression claims to have been Cleopatra or Henry VIII, which I know to be utterly untrue as the vast majority of my clients' past lives have been quite mundane - indeed in many cases quite boring.

So I suppose it was easier for me to simply ignore the occasional claims in the popular press that some celebrity or other had uncovered a past life as a great emperor or some such well known person from history, chuckling knowingly to myself that the egos of the rich and famous knew no bounds. After all, in the thousands of Past Life Regression sessions I'd completed, no-one had relived a past life of anyone remotely famous. And then…well, things began to change my viewpoint to such a degree, that here I am writing about people who I have regressed back into such famous past lives that even now my credulity is strained to its limits by the magnitude of the claims I'm making. This is because over a period of a few years clients came to me who in hypnosis regressed back into extremely famous previous lives.

In every case detailed in this book I had no idea when I first started working with these people that they had had such significant past lives. All but one of them came to me for therapy to help with their issues and in each case the information that came through in their hypnotherapy sessions came through quite spontaneously and was not suggested or implanted by me in any shape or form (that's another myth about hypnosis by the way, that everything is implanted by the therapist who is merely leading the client whilst they are in trance). The past life memories which they recounted to me whilst in trance surprised them as much as it amazed me. I can wholeheartedly state that in my opinion, supported by the experience of having conducted so many hypnotic regression sessions, that none of them were making it up or faking it in any way.

To stretch the bounds of belief even further I should mention that as well as the famous reincarnations described in the following pages, in my travels I have also met the reincarnation of Joan of Arc (who was so shocked when the memories came through - ironically enough in a smoking cessation session - that she refused to come back to explore it in more depth) and have heard of the reincarnation of Albert Einstein, who is currently a young autistic lad living in the North of England. I've also met the reincarnation of Baron von Richthofen -'the Red Baron'- living in Arizona, USA, and possibly a woman who relived the life of Queen Victoria during a workshop I ran in Nottingham a few years ago. I have also met, but not had chance to regress, a lady who was probably not just one of the Bronte sisters in her past life but all 3 of them - Charlotte, Emily and Anne (they appear to have been one soul divided into 3 lives on earth!).

Yes, I know these are whopping pieces of name-dropping and I can hardly believe them myself, and I have been wondering if the universe has been bringing these people to me for a reason, though what that reason is I find it hard to understand. Maybe the spiritual 'powers-that-be' want the concept of reincarnation to be publicised to a wider public so that people begin to be intrigued by the concept of past lives. Perhaps if people begin to believe in the reality of past and future lifetimes, this will help to create the spiritual shifts that are necessary at this crucial period in mankind's development. Some spiritual traditions say that we are currently standing at 'the razor's edge' where unless we raise our energy vibrations to a higher level, and do it very soon, we will enter a dark age in humankind's time here on earth. Living our present life in the knowledge that it will affect our future lives may be an essential part of that spiritual shift. I have heard it said by a Buddhist teacher that until mankind believes in reincarnation there will be no peace on earth.

Anyway, perhaps I should leave the esoteric philosophy to others more advanced spiritually. I can only report, honestly, on the things I have encountered since I first began working as a hypnotherapist in 1992.

I think it should also be stated at the outset, that all of the people whose past lives are reported in this book are normal, everyday people. None of them have any history of psychiatric illnesses or delusional tendencies. All but one of them came to me with issues they needed help with using hypnotherapy and all of them spontaneously accessed their famous past lives without any prompting from me. They were all just as surprised as I was with what came through in their sessions.

So, were they really reliving their previous lives as famous people, or were they imagining it all? Were they remembering stuff they had seen on TV or read in books? Were they opening up the Akashic Records of those people they claim to have been? Or is there some other explanation for what they experienced? I'll leave you to make up your own mind.

Chapter 2

The Power of Past Life Regression

Before I introduce you to the past life personalities I'd like to just 'pre-frame' everything by giving you some information on Past Life Regression and Reincarnation Therapy so that what follows makes more sense.

Let me start by saying a few words about hypnosis itself, since there are so many myths and misconceptions about it and it is widely misunderstood by the general public. Firstly, hypnosis is not some sort of sleep state. This mistaken belief has come about primarily because of stage hypnosis (which many hypnotherapists abhor) in which the stage hypnotist clicks his fingers and says "sleep" and the poor stooges on stage drop down into trance. However, those people are NOT asleep - if they were they obviously wouldn't hear the instructions given to them to make fools of themselves in various ways.

Neither is hypnosis a coma-type state or an experience similar to going under anaesthetic, where the person doesn't know what is happening to them or is powerless to go against the suggestions given by the hypnotherapist. It is not an experience where they lose control or where secrets are divulged without consent. All of these are myths, pure and simple.

The truth about hypnosis is that the hypnotic state is a state of relaxation. We all enter hypnosis several times each day, either when we daydream or when we allow ourselves to relax physically and mentally. In a hypnotic (or trance) state we are fully aware of everything that is taking place and we can hear sounds and noises around us and respond to them if we want to. We tend to become mentally more focussed on whatever is going on inside of us - feelings, thoughts, images etc., even though we are still aware of the Hypnotherapist's voice and can respond to it when necessary.

So, not sleep or coma, just a nice feeling of relaxed inner awareness where we are still in control and not under the control of the therapist. It is in this pleasant relaxation that we can be guided back through our memory banks into previous lives.

We often use the terms 'conscious' and 'subconscious' minds without always being aware of what the two terms mean. Our conscious mind is our thinking, analytical mind. As you are reading these words you are logically making sense of them using your conscious, thinking mind. If you imagine an iceberg, with its tip above the surface of the waves, that is the conscious part of our minds. Beneath the surface of the waves though, lays the vast bulk of the iceberg, which means that our subconscious mind is hidden beneath the thinking mind. I like to think of it as the 'engine room' of the mind. Our subconscious (or unconscious mind) controls our bodily functions like walking and breathing, and it contains our emotions, our intuition, and records of everything that has ever happened to us. In rough percentage terms, recent research suggests that our conscious mind contains less than 1% of our mental capabilities, whilst our subconscious is more than 99% of our mental powers. According to research quoted in 'The New Unconscious' (Editors: Hassin, Uleman and Bargh), whilst consciousness processes 50 bits of information per second, the rest of the brain processes 11 million bits per second!

As a hypnotherapist I use regression frequently as a means of helping my clients to heal a wide variety of issues. Regression simply means going back in our minds to relive memories of past events and hypnotherapists who have the ability and correct training use it regularly to guide clients back into SEE's (Significant Emotional Events) that have occurred earlier in this lifetime (usually childhood, at birth or in the womb before birth). The client usually experiences the negative emotions that have been locked into the subconscious mind from these events and releases them, often by crying, shaking or even screaming in some cases. Some clients gain a greater understanding of why they have had problems by gaining the knowledge of the causes of their problems (which can include negative patterns and behaviours) and these insights can allow deep, long-lasting healings to occur.

Some hypnotherapists also guide their clients back into past lives to clear present life blockages, and even fewer of us work on clearing ancestral, genetically inherited traumas to heal current life issues. Occasionally I have even been involved in future life progression, to look ahead into lifetimes to come!

It should be said that even within the hypnotherapy profession Past Life Regression and Reincarnation Therapy is still controversial with many hypnotherapists refusing to use it as a therapeutic tool. This, I have to say, amazes me as I have seen so many incredible healings over the years and I've completed so many past life sessions that have eradicated my client's problems that I firmly believe that Reincarnation Therapy should be regarded as a serious therapeutic discipline. My experience is that so many issues from which we suffer as human beings can stem from traumas or locked-in behaviour patterns from previous lifetimes.

Let me list just a few of the problems that may have their roots in former lives:

- Depression
- Anxieties and panic attacks
- Phobias and fears
- Skin problems
- Physical illnesses (including migraines, asthma and cancer)
- Lack of confidence and self-worth
- Sexual problems
- Alcohol and substance abuse

- Weight issues
- Behavioural problems
- Smoking addiction
- Stress
- Relationship challenges
- Pain

And many more too numerous to mention. The list is almost endless, but all significant 21st century ailments which inhibit us and which stop us from living our lives freely, joyfully and with a sense of inner peace could stem from events in previous lives.

Basically, many symptoms we have that usually end up with a trip to the GP have underlying emotional causes. My work as a therapist generally consists of finding and releasing the underlying emotion that has been locked in as a result of past traumas and then the issue, or symptom, can heal or reduce. Release the emotional driver that is fuelling the problem and then the energy goes out of it and the problem ceases to exist. It really is that simple. Reincarnation Therapy is 'Cause and Effect' therapy - uncover the cause and whatever is supporting the behaviour collapses and the effect is healed. There is a school of thought that ALL issues (yes, ALL issues) we have as human beings connect back to underlying emotional causes. Louise Hay, in her wonderful book 'You Can Heal Your Life', seems to support this view.

Although many therapy sessions with my clients over the years have become past life sessions, very few people come to me with either knowledge of, or a belief in, the subject of reincarnation. Still fewer feel that the cause of their issue is something that happened in a lifetime before this one. However, once they access trance in many, many cases their subconscious minds (the deep, inner mind in which all distant memories are stored) has guided them back to the source of their problems which is usually some trauma or series of traumas in previous lives. Often this is a death in a past life that has been so traumatic that its energy has been locked into the client's subconscious and carried with them into this present lifetime. The energy of that trauma then bubbles up under the surface of the conscious mind causing the issues which are blighting or limiting their lives. By re-experiencing the death or trauma in the past life (which can sometimes be quite dramatic but perfectly safe to go through provided the therapist is properly trained) the problem is healed.

There are those who mock or question the reality of the process but usually from a position of fear, ignorance or prejudice. I could write many pages detailing some of the hundreds of healings I've seen when using Past Life Therapy. However, I will simply state that if Past Life Therapy was not real it would not be happening so frequently in my sessions, and with such amazing results. People just keep getting better, often from issues or illnesses they had suffered from all their lives, regardless of whether they believe in the concept of past lives or not. I must say that most people who come to me for therapy do not believe in (or have any real knowledge of) reincarnation, but they still get better once they've relived their previous lives. The reality is that past lives cannot be just explained away simply as imaginary fantasies by those who experience them. This makes what follows all the more intriguing. So, without further ado, let me introduce you now to the first of the historical personages I've had the privilege to have encountered. Please note that all of my clients' names have been changed to preserve anonymity.

Chapter 3

A Woman in Love

Lisa is the only one of the clients in this book who did not come to me for help with a specific issue. She 'phoned me in a state of confusion, explaining that she had experienced a spontaneous flashback which she thought could be from a past life. This happened when she accidentally touched the hands of a man at work who she instinctively felt she knew, yet she had never really spoken in any real depth to before. As their hands touched in the office in which they worked, she began to have flashbacks in the form of images of herself sitting in a large hall in front of a big fireplace. She was wearing a large, long dress and sitting looking at a candlestick on a long, dark wood table. The floor had chequered tiles and she had rings on her fingers and beautiful red hair cascading on to her shoulders. Along with the images she felt a feeling of impatience, as though she were excitedly waiting for something or someone. She had then experienced a brief flash of being in bed with someone.

Lisa felt disturbed by the experience and wondered if they could be from another lifetime and also if the man at work – Tony - could have been with her in that life. She came to me with the express desire to find out more of what these images meant. This is pretty standard fare for me, as I have had the pleasure to work with a number of people who have had similar experiences. However, what came out in the session was totally unexpected when we began to realise just who the woman really was whom she had seen in her mind's eye sitting impatiently at that table in that old hall.

Lisa arrived for our first session feeling somewhat nervous and doubting herself in case the visions she had had proved to be just some sort of fantasy. An intelligent, articulate 28-year-old, she shared with me again the flashbacks and wondered if they were of any real significance. As we began hypnosis Lisa laid back, closed her eyes, and went readily and gently into trance. I guided her back into the past in her thoughts, moving back through her present life before taking her back into time before this life and then into the images she had been experiencing in the form of flashbacks. In a hushed voice she described being a young woman alone in a large, oak-panelled room, impatiently waiting for someone to come:

SB: "How are you feeling?"

L: "I'm fidgety and restless. I don't know why they aren't coming to tell me that he's here"

SB: "Who are you waiting for?"

L: "I'm thinking about a man with dark hair and a beard wearing dark green. When I think about him looking at me I feel all nice and warm inside. I wish he was here. I feel almost cross. I can hear my dress rustling and my fingernails impatiently tapping. He's been away - why isn't he coming? I want him to come."

It was the first (and certainly not the last) time in our sessions that Lisa's manner changed. As she relived being the woman she became imperious as she spoke and her manner became quite haughty. Then, she softened:

"I'm in a different room now. In a bedroom with dark wood-panelling all around. He's here beside me - we're in bed together. I can hear giggling outside the door. I'm laughing too. He's got his shirt undone and I feel very happy but also naughty. I hope no-one comes looking for me. We're talking - he's holding my hand and stroking my face. I'm looking into his dark eyes. I wish we could stay like this but I know I have to get back. There's giggling and whispering outside the door. I've a good mind to tell them off but I'm not properly dressed. They mustn't see me like this."

The scene then changed to a large room with pillars and pennants hanging down the walls and hundreds of smartly dressed people around her:

> *"I'm in the middle but no-one stands near me. An old man is being polite to me. The man I know is in front of me - I can see people watching him intently. I'm wearing a white glove and he's holding my hand and kissing it as he bows reverentially. I feel important."*

After a pause, during which she seemed to be listening to what was being said around her, she suddenly said the words which took this from being just another ordinary past life session for me into something which had me sitting bolt upright in my chair:

> *"The old man's calling me 'your Majesty'. I feel happy but sad at the same time because I know that because of who I am I can't be with him. I have to be alone and he knows it too but I long to be with him."*

At this point Lisa became emotional and as she cried she gave a further hint as to the personalities that she was revealing:

> *"It doesn't seem fair that I can't have him. He calls me 'Bess' when we're alone - he says I am his. He's Robert. He likes it when I say his name. He feels he belongs to me. People are cheering for me and I feel shy, but I feel resigned that we cannot be together."*

Lisa gradually composed herself and moved to another scene, in which she realised that Robert in the past life is Tony in this one, the touch of whose hands had sparked off the flashbacks in the first place:

> *"I'm sitting by a river at a party, laughing. There's music and jollity. I'm surrounded by people but I'm looking for Robert. I'm*

wearing black with silver and pearls - I like pearls. The sun's going down. I see him" (she smiles and softens in the chair) *"and he doffs his hat to me. I smile but I have to smile to myself because of the people there. He is my lover, a lord from a long line of titles. He is Dudley, Earl of Leicester. We are very close and he is as much to me as he could be, we know each other so well but there has to be limits."*

We finished the session and Lisa surfaced from trance, shocked by what she had experienced. "Could this be real?" she asked hesitantly, because the implication that she could be the reincarnation of Queen Elizabeth I seemed so extraordinary. We talked about it and I admitted that I had to remain sceptically open-minded until we knew more about it. We both agreed to do more sessions in order to see if what she'd relived was just confabulated memories based on something she'd read in a book or seen on TV, or if she could come up with further detailed memories that would confirm the truth about what had happened in the session.

As I have a sceptical nature I did feel suspicious however, but when I questioned her as to whether she'd read much about Elizabeth, Lisa assured me that she had not. Although she had visited some historical sites in the past she felt that she probably knew no more about her than anybody of average education in the UK. She did admit, though, to feeling dumbfounded at what she'd seen and felt. That made two of us then!

Chapter 4

Reality Bites

A few days later Lisa emailed me, sharing her continuing astonishment, and telling me that after the session she had had further flashbacks into the life which just came through spontaneously when she was doing everyday things. It appeared that the door in her mind behind which the memories had lain dormant and hidden was now partially open and further insights and memories from the past life continued to emerge in her waking hours. This became a feature of the process throughout the time that we worked together, with Lisa uncovering memories in our hypnosis sessions and afterwards having other visions which came into her mind all by themselves.

She wrote:

It was good to meet you on Tuesday and the session was certainly interesting! I spent the rest of the day and part of the following one feeling a bit dumbfounded. Since the session a few other things have come to light....I have had a snatch of a memory whereby I was standing in a chapel. It was lit by candles and the walls were painted with richly coloured and gilt frescoes. I saw the edge of a surface draped in white cloth. I am a little girl, not more than 9, and I am wearing a long dress in a dark colour. I have something on my head, a sort of cap thing and carrying a small book, bound in dark leather.

Then I saw in my mind's eye Traitor's Gate at the Tower of London. When I visited it last summer I was drawn inexplicably to it but when I got there I was transfixed with a sort of intense fear and loathing. Not sure if it's connected, but I've always had a fear and loathing of small rowing boats and dark water. Last time I got in one

I screamed a lot and was terrified the whole time. I also hate confined spaces related to water, such as canal locks where you have the slippery stone and the still, deep water. Some of the buildings in the Tower also drew me, but unfortunately they are the ones to which the public don't have access. This was all before the memories that we explored.

I haven't really had much exposure to Elizabeth I or information relating to her. I have never studied her at school, or until last year, visited any properties related to her. When I visited Hatfield the old palace is the one that grabbed me. [The Royal Palace of Hatfield was the childhood home and favourite residence of Elizabeth. It was pulled down and rebuilt after her death, but ruins of the old palace still remain]. *I remember feeling extremely frustrated at not being able to get into the smaller, older building next to the main palace. Standing outside it felt like home. Elizabeth has always stood out for me though, like a highlighted word. I have always felt a sort of tingle when I've seen pictures of her.*

One other thing. Whilst at Kenilworth (and I swear I didn't know the link until I left the site and actually read the guidebook!) I had the oddest feeling of coming back to a treasured place, somewhere familiar that I was fond of. [Kenilworth, in Warwickshire, was given to Robert Dudley, Earl of Leicester by Elizabeth and she visited him here several times]. *I was drawn to Leicester's building and stood staring at it. Somehow I knew what it looked like. The place for me had a tangible, lovely atmosphere and I was loathe to leave it. I heard of a fireplace that had been taken from the old building built by Leicester that was now in the gatehouse. In my mind I could clearly see it. Later I walked past a board containing a photo of the fireplace and was surprised to see a photo of the image I had in my mind! Something happened in front of that fireplace and as I thought of it my body was tingly. I have since mentioned this to Tony and he explained that he has experienced something similar with the fireplace and has a strong sense of home whilst in the castle grounds.*

In her next visit to me I deliberately said little once Lisa was in trance, allowing her subconscious to take her anywhere in that life, partly as a means of building a more complete picture of this apparent life of a Queen, and partly as an attempt to trip her up. By doing this my intention was to see if she came up with anything that felt unreal or untrue in relation to Elizabeth's life, which would suggest that what she had been seeing was not real. This, however, did not happen and the memories which she relived proved to be just as fascinating as her first time, full of small, peculiar details that suggested to me the veracity of what was coming through from her subconscious.

This time we began with some childhood memories before moving into events that had a profound impact upon Princess Elizabeth. After talking me through some pleasant memories of her father, King Henry VIII, and of spending time in a chapel as a girl with her governess, Lisa went silent for a while as her subconscious took her to a time in her late teens. As she lay in trance her body began to stiffen in the chair and her face became set and fearful.

> L: *"I can see spikes on a portcullis set in an arch. It's low and wide and cold and dark. I'm in a tiny boat and I can hear water lapping onto some steps."*
> SB: "How do you feel?"
> *"I'm scared and I want to go home. There's a woman with me. I can see her and men waiting for me with torches. I know I shouldn't be here. I step out of the tiny boat and I'm standing at the bottom of the steps. Water's wetting my dress and I'm hugging my arms around me. The woman's talking to me, calling me 'princess' and trying to persuade me I must go. She says 'it's worse to do as you do now'."*

During this scene Lisa had begun to shiver and shake, feeling the cold and darkness of what was obviously her water-borne entry into the Tower of London, and obviously fearful of Elizabeth's predicament. This is a common feature of regression sessions, where the person in trance relives the physical and emotional feelings from the past as if it were happening in the present. Lisa continued:

> "I don't want to go into that place. I can hear keys. She's talking to me - I know I have to go. I walk up the steps and into a courtyard, there are lots of torches and people in corners watching and whispering. I know some think me guilty."

Lisa's quivering intensified her whole body rigid as she felt Elizabeth's terror at finding herself in this place. Historians have written of the profound effect that this episode in Elizabeth's life had upon her. It appears that throughout her imprisonment in the Tower she lived constantly in fear of her life, expecting daily to be executed for her alleged part in a plot against her elder sister Mary. By her own admission her three months incarceration was the most traumatic event of her youth. Historical accounts show that later in life Elizabeth said 'I stood in danger of my life; my sister was so incensed against me' and she viewed her safe deliverance as a miracle, ceaselessly giving thanks to God and composing prayers of praise for 'pulling me from the prison to the palace'. As we shall see later, Queen Mary reappears in Lisa's regressions with a surprising twist.

Lisa continued with her story, her eyes closed but her whole body showing the agitation of Elizabeth's trauma, her voice now down to a whisper:

> "I can hear keys. The door's unlocked and then slammed behind me. I'm inside a cold, dark, dank room. My lady's taken her wrap off her head. I don't know whether I feel more angry or scared. I know I am here unjustly."

After a pause, she began to relax and her body softened, her features letting go of the tension and it became obvious that she had moved on to another less threatening scene:

"I'm sitting in the shade of a huge tree in new leaf - I like to sit here. I can hear people calling my name. A man's in front of me, he goes down on one knee and he's holding something at me - it's a ring. I know what it means - Mary's gone."

SB: "How do you feel?"

"A little daunted, a little overwhelmed. All those who never knelt to me before are kneeling. Excited too, but perfectly aware of the gravity of the situation. They're shouting my name because she's dead. I'm not sure how long I'm supposed to stand while they kneel." Lisa laughed at this, feeling Elizabeth's slight embarrassment, then continued:

"So I am Queen even though it's a heavy duty to bear. I think of my father, who I don't think expected this to happen. I hear bells starting to ring, far away. Everyone knows who I am. I know things won't ever be the same again."

All of this was spoken in a totally unselfconscious way by Lisa, who was reliving Elizabeth's accession to the throne upon Mary's death as if she was actually there, sitting under a tree in an English courtyard or garden and feeling the full weight of responsibility fall upon her shoulders. As if to know some relief from this burden and to enjoy some pleasure after the earlier horrors of the Tower the next scene that we moved on to was of happier things, a banquet at court with Robert Dudley:

"I'm in a large chamber, in the middle of a top table laid out for a feast. So much food! Fruit piled up on a platter and I have a silver cup with wine in it. It's all very lavish. Cloths on the tables are burgundy with gold decorations. I can hear pipe or flute music. I can also hear my ladies giggling and gossiping as they look at the men around me. I can see Robin - that's what I call him anyway. [This appears to have been Elizabeth's pet name for Robert Dudley, although

throughout our sessions she would call him Robert, Leicester, Dudley as well as Robin]. *He's on the opposite side of the room to me. I have to remember I can't stare at him. People are dancing - wherever there's a gap we smile at each other. No-one will know, they'll think we're smiling at the dancing. I guess I'm in my early 20's."*

After a pause, she continued excitedly, describing an episode which is reminiscent of the ballroom scene in the movie West Side Story, in which the two lovers only have eyes for each other in the midst of a crowd of people:

"He's coming over. I'm trying hard not to smile. He asks if I will dance. Lots of people gasp when I stand up to do so. I think to myself let them stare, then I scold myself for forgetting who I am. I dance - everyone stops and it's just me and him. People are whispering. What do I care what they think? He's smiling. I look into his eyes. I feel so happy it's as if people around us have ceased to exist - it's just us. I concentrate utterly upon him." Lisa sighed deeply at this point, the bitter-sweetness of Elizabeth's feelings overwhelming her.
"There's always the thought that it can only be so limited so we have to make the most of little moments like that. I feel free when I dance with him - I want it to go on forever. My ladies are watching me. I don't care, it's my time with him."

The scene faded and after a pause Lisa moved to earlier, childhood memories in which she correctly remembered the name of her governess, Kat Ashley and the fond feelings she had for her, and waiting in a candle-lit chapel to give her father the gift of a little book she had made for him.

The session ended and once more I found myself feeling baffled as to the reality of all this. Nothing she had remembered contradicted anything that is commonly known about Elizabeth's life and everything fitted in. We both agreed it was all fascinating if a bit hard to take in. Could Lisa really be the reincarnation of Elizabeth I?

Chapter 5

Deeper and Deeper

A few days later Lisa again emailed me with more recollections which had come through after the session. She wrote:

> *I keep seeing Robert Dudley's face in my mind's eye and feeling a mixture of distress and disappointment. Also, I see him stood before a fireplace with his hand resting on the mantle-shelf. He's looking up at me and we stand very close together - I think we are in private. I feel a sense of elation followed by a horrible sense of deflation and responsibility.*

She also remembered images of an important state occasion in a cathedral or church.

> *I was walking down the aisle wearing long, heavy robes that were heavily embroidered and I could feel them trailing behind me. I saw a chair on a raised platform and as I reached the chair I turned to sit down and felt the robes fold around my legs as I did so. My hair was long and brushed to be shiny, left entirely loose on my shoulders. When I looked up and in front of me there were hundreds of people, watching me. I could see two Bishops, one stood to either side of me, and I felt nervous and excited at the same time.*

These memories of what could be the coronation felt significant so in our next session together, once Lisa was in trance, I asked her to go to the day of the coronation. Her voice trembled a little as she described the scene:

"I'm standing at the back of the Abbey and can see row upon row of people in front of me. There's a fantastic atmosphere, and pennants hanging down from the tops of pillars. They're placing heavy, embroidered robes on me and I feel nervous but excited. I move up the centre aisle and I can feel the robe dragging heavily behind me. I'm focussing on the chair ahead of me - it's raised up - and can hear music and a choir singing. People are wearing lavish clothes. It seems to take forever to walk up the aisle. I sit down and place my arms on the arms of the chair. There are members of the clergy - bishops - on either side of me and everyone's staring at me. Dudley's there too, sat to my left, watching me. He's dressed in dark green. I can't smile. I feel nervous as I see the crown - there's no going back once they give it to me. The bishop's bringing the crown down onto my head. There's a feeling like electricity going down my spine. I turn my hands over to receive the sceptre. It feels cold where it's been sat on the cushion. In the other hand I have an orb. People are smiling, some are applauding. The music's back - they're singing songs for me. I stand for the first time as the Queen. Every last person bows to me. I walk back down the aisle and as I pass each row they bow whilst trying hard to look at me. At the end of the aisle an adviser introduces me to people I must meet. Before I do that, Dudley's in front of me - he's skirted around. I offer him my hand and he bows and kisses it. I'm pleased he's come to me. He backs quickly away. A lot of people are standing around but they don't come close to me. I stand in the middle of them with Lord Cecil talking to me quietly, telling me what I have to do. I see sunlight through the top windows of the Abbey, making a pool of colour. It's a beautiful day. The door opens and I hear terrific shouting from outside and bells ringing, so loud. They've taken off the robe. That feels better. I walk to the door with Cecil at my side and Dudley skirting round pillars and smiling at me. I go through the door and there are thousands shouting. I feel so humble that so many people have come to see me. I'm helped into a carriage at the bottom of the steps and I try to look round to see everyone waving as we pull away."

Personally, I love the way that amidst all that pomp and ceremony there is the human touch of Dudley, like a lovesick teenager, trying to catch her eye as she walks in procession through the Abbey. As if to emphasise this, Lisa's next memory in the session was a touching one, of just her and Dudley enjoying moments of deep love and togetherness.

"I'm in a meadow with small white flowers in long grass. I'm sat in the grass laughing till I fall over backwards. Robert's with me - he's laughing as well. He's been chasing me. We sit together, laughing and smiling at each other. It feels warm. I can see two horses tethered to a tree, the grey one's mine. His is dark brown with a beautiful cherry-red saddle. I see a pheasant slung over the back of his horse - we've been hunting. He gazes at me. Sometimes we don't need to say anything.

He looks so deep into my eyes. We're clutching hands. I feel wonderful. I love him so much. We've found a little time to be alone. I know he loves me too. His touch is so gentle, he trails his fingers over my hand and up my arms and into my hair. He loves it when I wear it loose. I don't want this moment to end. Then he kisses me. I certainly don't want that to stop. We sit with our foreheads and noses touching and I feel as though no-one could ever separate us. We were with a hunting party. I can hear people and horses in the distance. I feel annoyed because I know it'll have to end - again. We stand up and dust the grass off. I straighten my hair and compose myself. It's a sad end to this intimacy, which is so rare. I feel it in Robert. He hangs his head. He helps me onto my horse and by the time the others get to us it appears that we've just been a little way ahead of them, though some of them watch us and they know. I spur my horse on and its fast galloping makes me feel better. They follow me with Dudley riding behind me to the right."

The unsatisfactory nature of her love affair with Dudley came over strongly in several of our sessions, with Elizabeth torn between her yearning to openly acknowledge Robert as her lover and to enjoy a normal, loving relationship with him, and the ever-present demands of State and the impossibility of her position as Queen marrying a commoner. It's as if all the time her love for Dudley was tempered by sadness and heartache. This inner agony became more intense in a later session, which was so painful and emotional to Lisa as she experienced it that she actually stopped the hypnosis and came out of trance because she felt so distressed:

> "I'm alone, holding a book and sitting on the grass in the middle of a small rectangular garden. I can smell lavender. I'm reading quietly and no-one disturbs me. I'm wearing pearls and am distractedly twisting them around my finger. I'm day-dreaming about Robert. It's some time after we've separated. I remember how warm and content I used to feel in his company, how we used to ride, the times we used to laugh out loud when no-one was around and then he'd grab me and hold me and make me laugh all the more. Then a cloud comes across the sun and jolts me out of it. The warm content feelings are gone and I feel tense and frowning, knowing that I can't give in to my grief. I pick up my book and stand up and walk out of the garden. I feel cold. I can't feel the warmth of the sun anymore."

With this unconscious metaphor of the loss of her love Lisa began to cry, her face contorted in anguish as she felt all of the locked-in pain of Elizabeth's broken heart. She sobbed violently as one who has just lost the love of their life, releasing the emotion that Elizabeth herself had not been allowed to release. After some minutes of this, as if unable to bear the pain any longer Lisa brought herself out of trance and sat crying for some time. Once she had composed herself she agreed to go back into trance and I asked her to go back to her first meeting with Robert. This time she remembered things a little more from a distance, as if to stay separate from the emotions of what she was recounting:

"I'd known him for a long time, since I was a child; it's so hard to say when things change. Long before I'm crowned I start to notice him. Things became more intense in my mid-20's I think. It carries on then very intensely for maybe 5-6 years after I'm crowned then it feels as if there was a lull. Something else was happening and there are just odd occasions when we're together and when we are we're reminded that our feelings have to buried. Things go flat after Kenilworth - we correspond but things are not the same. It's after he proposes to me. I feel it was unfair because I can't do that. I chose to distance myself after that."

For some reason, perhaps because the pain of certain aspects of Elizabeth's life were resonating inside Lisa, her subconscious then took her into the other major trauma of the Queen's life:

"I can see a tall narrow doorway with huge black bolts on it. It's dark and the wood is old, dry and brittle and there are heavy stone walls. I can hear people screaming far away. I feel afraid. I know this place." Lisa's face turned white, her features tense and pinched and her breathing quickened. She shivered. I asked her how she felt. *"Very anxious and cross. I oughtn't to be here. They're wrong bringing me here. I stand accused of treason against Mary. They're quite wrong, but I worry they will find some way of proving I'm at fault. They killed my mother here. I'm afraid the same will befall me. I can't settle, I'm pacing up and down. It's a narrow room, a little wider towards the end. There's a plate with bread on it and a candle. I hear people pass the door outside and the sound of keys. I hear the bolts slide back and keys in the lock and the door swings open. There are three of them there and they command me to come with them like a criminal, which I am not. I feel so afraid. Am I to be questioned or be killed? I straighten myself up and look them straight in the eyes. They flank me as we go down a dark passage. One of them wears dark blue - he is old. We go into an empty, dusty room and they shut the door and light some candles.*

They ask me to take a chair but they stand and look at me coldly, as if they hate me. They say they come on the orders of Mary. They fire questions at me and try to put words into my mouth." Lisa's voice became hard with anger at this point. *"I know I am innocent and did not do the things with which they charge me. I clench my hands together. They pace the room and fire accusations. My answers fall on deaf ears. I will not admit guilt to a charge which I know is not justified."* After a pause Lisa went on. *"They have exhausted their incessant questioning and I am taken back down the passage into my prison room. I feel my anger rising but they shut the door as I whirl round to confront them. I'm shaking, angry but relieved I haven't died this night. I sit on the edge of a low, pallet-like bed and wait. In the morning I hear people outside again and I stand ready for them. The nobles from last night come into my cell and tell me I am to be freed - if you can call it freedom. I'm to be taken to Hatfield and kept there until I hear otherwise. I'm not allowed to leave the estate. I feel relief I can go. I long to see Robert."*

Who knows the terror the young princess must have felt when her gaolers came to open her door on the morning after her interrogation? Was she to be executed like her mother? Throughout the above experience Lisa's body was stiff and tense as she relived the fear Elizabeth must have felt. After all this distress her mind gave her what she wanted and she was taken to a happier memory which she felt took place shortly after her release from the Tower.

"I'm in a long, narrow hall with windows high up in the walls and exposed timbers. I'm surrounded by ladies and we're dancing in lines. We whirl round and clap - it's terribly precise - you have to know what you're doing or someone will fall over you. It feels wonderful to be free to dance again. It's soon after my release. One of the ladies keeps looking to the doorway. A servant enters and bows low to me, telling me that Robert's here. I reach out a hand behind

me and a lady takes it and squeezes it. The ladies fall back and there he is. I smile and he smiles at me. I cross the room, trying not to run. I'm so glad.

The ladies are amused. We step outside, just us, into a little garden. When we're sure no-one watches he holds me so tightly. He strokes my hair and says my name over and over. I feel safe and a surge of relief to see him. We walk a little and then sit amongst the flowers as we talk. I cry about what has happened and he cups my face in his hands and reminds me of who I am. When he smiles at me it's like the warmth of the sun. I bask in the warmth of him.

He reminds me I have friends who will remain beside me, and then kisses the back of my neck and buries his nose in my hair. Someone brings us wine. It's always so brief when I see him. I wish it didn't have to end but we treasure our meetings. I feel sad about what will be - no matter what we feel for each other we'll never be together."

The session ended and an exhausted Lisa came back to full awareness, her energies spent after the rigours of everything she had experienced. I should say that the level of the emotion people so often experience in past life sessions cannot be conjured up or faked. The intensity in some sessions is so incredibly profound both for me to witness and for my clients to experience. Many people say they are overwhelmed by the feelings. These deep and intense levels of emotion are one way in which we can assess the reality of the client's responses during regression.

It was about this time that I began to read a couple of biographies on Elizabeth in order to check if any of the details which she recounted could be corroborated. I was pleasantly surprised to find that much of what Lisa had said was factually correct. The name of Lord Cecil (whom she had mentioned during the coronation scene as talking to her and guiding her) was a historical fact, as William Cecil, 1st Lord of Burghley, was her chief adviser and good friend for the next forty years after she was crowned as Queen. I'm not sure that anyone who has not researched or read about Elizabeth's life and reign would have known this was the case. Lisa assured me that she had not begun to read anything about Elizabeth since we had been working together, so other than a couple of visits in the past to castles associated with Elizabeth she really knew very little about Elizabeth's life. So how did she know this fact about Lord Cecil?

Chapter 6

Glimpses of Elizabeth

So many different things about Elizabeth's life came through in our sessions that after a while I began to soften my initial scepticism. It started to dawn on me that I was beginning to believe in the truth of the information coming through in the sessions and in the likelihood that Lisa was indeed Elizabeth I in a previous life. The scope of what Lisa recounted was so wide-ranging and sometimes so detailed that I could no longer contemplate that she was imagining it all. As well as this, quite often in hypnosis she would take on the manner and imperiousness of the Queen. Many times Lisa experienced Elizabeth's feelings and exhibited them in such a way that suggested to me that she was indeed experiencing her life and emotions. This is something that I often see in Past Life Regression sessions. I can honestly state that, in my opinion as a facilitator of thousands of Past Life Regressions, she was not acting these out consciously but really reliving past experiences which had lain dormant in her subconscious for most of her life, until the touch of Tony's hand acted like a catalyst and triggered the doors in her mind to begin opening.

Before I continue with the details of Elizabeth's relationship with Dudley, including some intimate moments they enjoyed together (as well as stunning confirmation of rumours that circulated about the relationship in Elizabeth's lifetime), I'd like to share with you some other aspects of her life that Lisa remembered in our meetings.

Although Elizabeth's conflict with Mary Queen of Scots has been well documented over the centuries, it only came through fleetingly in Lisa's regressions. However, it was clear that the situation regarding Mary troubled the Queen, who only signed her death warrant reluctantly. Initially, the subject of Mary Stuart came through whilst Lisa was reliving one of Elizabeth's summer encampments at the home of one of her nobles. The problem of what to do about Mary must have been on her mind as she travelled the country:

> "I can see a church in a village. All the houses are built in a pale, sandy stone. I think it's Fotheringhay. I can hear church bells ringing. I've just arrived. People are standing along the road."
> SB: "How old are you?"
> "I'm about 30-ish. I'm tired from travelling but glad to be here as it's a very pleasant place. I'm staying with a local family in a big house near the church. On the right of where I'm staying is a castle on the banks of the river. It's relaxing, away from the state palaces. I can be me here. I look around and see people watching me, awestruck. I still find that humbling. I go to the big house where my host lives with his family - I think there are 2 or 3 children. He has a grey beard and wears a dark brown velvet over-jacket and a funny flat hat. He's kind but jittery around me. I think his name is William. There's a table laden with food, fruit and wine in the house.
> I feel sombre somehow, as if there's a weight on me. I'm thinking about my cousin, Mary Stuart. She's been plotting and my advisers urge me to arrest her but no-one has found a suitable venue in which she could be held. This is perfect, it seems a pleasant place for her to be imprisoned. The thought of sending her to the Tower is repugnant to me. I don't want to imprison one of my own family, but I don't have a choice as she's too much of a threat."

In another session the sealing of Mary's fate came through:

> "I'm indoors in a big room. There are a lot of people standing around in front of me in a semicircle. I have a large piece of parchment, something I must sign but I'm hesitating. They're all men, urging

me to sign but I feel rushed. It's Mary's death warrant. I sign it and fold it over and smooth it flat, wondering if I've done the right thing. I smell wax melting. Someone prepares it for the seal. I stamp my seal down on it. A man takes it from me as I hold it out. I'm not sure I share their relief. I dismiss them all and look outside - it's a fine day with sun coming in through the high windows. I sit at my desk and clasp my hands in front of me, looking down at my fingers. I have a heavy feeling in the pit of my stomach."

A few days later Lisa emailed me with some further details which had come through to her after the session:

With regard to Mary Stuart's death warrant, I can tell you quite specifically that there was a condition to it. I was very reluctant to let it go even once I signed it, and I stated that Mary was to be executed in the great hall of Fotheringhay Castle, and not outside in the courtyard. She is to die inside.

Once more, Lisa had unknowingly got more information completely correct. Elizabeth prevaricated for the whole of 1586, fighting against the intense pressure coming from her advisors and Parliament to have Mary Queen of Scots put to death. Her utter reluctance to sign Mary's death warrant caused her great agony. It is said that the stress brought her close to a breakdown. Eventually, on 1st February 1587, she finally gave in and signed the warrant, stipulating that Mary was to be executed inside the Great Hall of Fotheringhay and not outside in the courtyard.

A feature of Lisa's sessions was the way in which she would move, in a disconnected way, through memories from different times in Elizabeth's life. Usually, once I had taken her into trance and guided her back into the past life, I let her subconscious take over and lead us wherever it wanted to go. Scenes from childhood, for example, would sometimes pop up in the middle of later experiences. I found some of these quite touching:

"I'm holding hands with my brother Edward. I'm very fond of him - he's a gentle child. He died young. Sometimes he'd call me 'Bessie' as it was easier than trying to say my name properly. I feel he wasn't very energetic. He didn't run around as much as I did."

SB: "What do you remember of your father?"

"He would take me walking in his garden and throw me little smiles. He was big and strong. After my mother died I saw less of him. Mother was very beautiful and had mischief in her dark eyes. She was so young when she died. I remember her in the garden with box hedges behind her. She's wearing a black hood with a pearl trim. She has clever eyes, an almond shaped face with a pointed chin and a delicate mouth. A chain around her neck has the letter 'B' on it. She's holding her hands out to me - I'm only small. Someone calls her from a large building. She doesn't look back at me, just hitches up her skirt and runs across the lawn. A servant woman picks me up. I didn't see her again - she died soon after that."

SB: "How do you feel about her?"

"Remote from her. I didn't know her that well. I knew the servants better than I knew her. I remember her necklace, with little pearls or beads hanging from the letter 'B'.

After a short pause she moved into a further early memory:

"Father's standing, singing, in the middle of a large room with a lot of people. There's a lot of noise with people talking and laughing. I can just hear music - flutes or pipes and a lute. Father is so much taller than most of them. I hear him laughing, a great, deep growl of a laugh. I'm about 5 or 6 years old. There's a young, pretty woman who people are watching. She's flirting to a circle of men around her. Father turns to look at her - I can tell he likes her. She's called Katherine. When father looks at her she becomes demure, coy and ladylike, as if she's showing off to get his attention. I watch for a while, then I feel bored so I thread my way out...now I'm lying in bed with people looking down at me, concerned and whispering.

Everything's blurry. I feel hot and unable to move. Someone puts something cool on my forehead. I don't want it but I'm too weak to stop them. They all seem so worried. I can see Mary. We're both children and she's jumping around in front of me. She's bossy and impatient and I feel quite irritated by her. She's gabbling on about something"

Elizabeth's love of music and dancing is well known, though like any modern teenager lessons often get in the way of having fun:

"We're dancing, a lot of us together. I'm in my teens. My hair's loose and it's getting in the way a bit. I'm dancing a Volta (what the heck's one of those - the word's just come into my mind?). My hair keeps smacking me in the face as I twirl. I'm clapping as I turn. I feel that this one's my favourite. An older lady is watching and she's held her hands up and clapped and we've stopped. I have to go to my lessons. I'm in a room with a globe and I have a quill pen, an inkwell and a long sheet of parchment on the table in front of me. Trying not to get ink on my fingers. My writing's neat. I sign my name with a flourish and seal a private letter with wax. There's a coat of arms above the fire and I feel comfortable in this room, as if I spend a lot of time here."

A Volta, by the way, was an energetic form of dance much beloved by Elizabeth. Lisa's questioning of the word whilst in trance is a good indication of the fact that when we are in a hypnotic trance our conscious mind is still operating and aware of everything that is happening to us. As I stated at the beginning of this book, hypnosis is not sleep or being in a coma. Quite often in regression sessions my clients will be experiencing past life memories and at the same time they will ask me questions about what is happening to them.

This triggered more recollections from Lisa, who continued to experience spontaneous mini-regressions (at home) after each session. She emailed me a few days after the above session:

I went to see the new Harry Potter film. The soundtrack contains a lot of Tudor/Elizabethan sounding music with tabors and flutes etc. As I was walking out of the auditorium I had the most overwhelming urge to start dancing! I felt a surge of euphoria as if I wanted to start a particularly energetic type of dancing. I had a flash of being in a long full gown, like the memory we found last time of dancing at court. As I strode across the foyer I looked down and saw myself wearing such a gown, darted in tightly at the waist, corset, bodice and long sleeves with a high, ornate lace collar. I could feel pearls on my ears and my dress was heavily embroidered brocade in a silvery gold colour with crimson, green, blue and gold floral embroidery. There were strings of pearls around my neck and some on the dress, which were swinging and hitting me as I walked. I could feel my hair all gathered up and piled on top of my head and I felt very decisive, as if I was on my way to do something important.

An image that I think we all have of Elizabeth is of the strong, nationalistic monarch holding firm to the reins of power. A scene which epitomises this patriotic strength was triggered for Lisa in which she could actually smell the sea in another memory. Having seen herself posing for an artist painting her portrait (I wonder if this was the famous Armada portrait painted after the victory against the Spanish?) Lisa moved to a memory in which she is rallying her troops and inspiring them with her words:

"I'm sitting in a long, rectangular room, near a small table, posing with my right hand on a globe. I'm in the light near a small, leaded glass window up to the right. I can smell paint and there's a man behind an easel in front of me. No-one's speaking. I'm wearing black, with a high collar and ruff, and pale pink bows and pearls on the dress. I have pearls in my hair too and several strands around my neck. I think some of the pearls may have been gifts. I'm in my 50's

I think and I feel bored as I can't move or talk. I can hear the sea and smell it too." This moved Lisa onto another scene:

"I'm stood looking towards the sea, or at least towards a wide stretch of water. I'm high up and there are ships moored below. There's a sea of faces, hundreds of men looking up towards me. It's overcast. There are a lot of people behind me too. I'm addressing them. I'm speaking of my strength as a monarch despite my status as a woman, of my love for England. I want her defended well. I'm asking them to defend her well against the Spanish. I'm putting a lot of emphasis into the words, to defend the country I love. I'm particularly aware of one man standing to my right. He's wearing blue with a handsome face and beard and he has a pearl drop hanging from his left ear. I think he's Raleigh and he will lead them. He seems determined to hold my gaze as I move away. It's started to rain."

Could Lisa have been remembering the famous day in August 1588 when the Queen in the midst of the crisis of the invasion by the Spanish Armada, went to Tilbury and gave the most famous speech of her reign? Dressed in a silver breastplate, "most bravely mounted on a most stately steed" and dressed as "an armed Pallas" according to contemporary accounts (how I wish I'd known this at the time of the session as I could have asked Lisa to describe her clothing etc) she used words which "inflamed the hearts of her good subjects", words which resounded around the land for years afterwards:

"I know I have the body of a weak and feeble woman, but I have the heart and stomach of a king, and a king of England too."

As Lisa recounted her memory in depth I could almost smell the salt air too and hear the pennants fluttering in the wind.

Chapter 7

Memories of Mary

We've already seen one result of Elizabeth's difficult relationship with her elder sister, Queen Mary, when she was falsely imprisoned in the Tower living in constant fear for her life. In one of our sessions I asked Lisa, whilst in trance, to specifically focus on memories of Mary, in order to build a more complete picture of their relationship. Having done that I again sat back and allowed Lisa's subconscious to take her where it wanted. As I've mentioned earlier, at no time did I lead Lisa or implant any memories into her mind. She became an older Elizabeth, looking back wistfully on their troubled times together. Firstly, however, she went into a slightly disconcerting memory where as an adolescent she was being groped by a middle-aged nobleman:

"I'm with Thomas Seymour in a large room, a library. He's standing very close to me, closer than I like him to be. I can feel his breath. He's got his hand on my back to stop me from moving away. It's just us two. I feel slightly afraid. He's very flushed in the face - he's trying to kiss me. I'm turning my face away, I don't want him to. I'm in my early teens, about 14 or 15. He's got a wild look in his eyes, as if he's determined to violate me in some way. I feel panicky. Someone opens the door - it's my stepmother Katherine. She looks astonished and puts her hands up to her face. He steps back and lets me go. I don't know whether to say something or run. She stands in the doorway and doesn't know what to say."

The embarrassment of the situation for all concerned is plain to see, in a scene which is more akin to something from a modern-day soap opera than life at court. I have checked in several books

about Elizabeth written by historians and found to my astonishment that in her teens Elizabeth was indeed harassed by
Thomas Seymour who enjoyed daily romps with her. These
would often take place whilst she lay in bed, with Seymour
coming into her room in his nightclothes. Queen Katherine
eventually became so concerned with his flirtations that she had
him sent away from court. Once more Lisa was recalling information which she was unlikely to have known from her cursory
knowledge of Tudor history.

After this Lisa moved into memories of Mary, memories
which are tinged with sadness and show a human side to the
Queen and her sense of loss over the way her relationship with
her half-sister turned sour:

*"Mary's got a smug, irritating grin on her face. I'm quite sure I
don't know what she's so pleased about. She's wearing a fawn-
coloured, velvet-type dress and has her hands clasped in her sleeves.
I feel irritated. When she smiles her eyes look calculating and cold.
We're both quite young, and it's as if we're facing each other out in
some way. She's laughing at me."* After a short pause, she
continued: *"I'm thinking now about being held in the Tower later
on and I feel angry that I wasn't granted an audience. She's put me
here on the grounds of hearsay. She won't let me explain I wasn't
involved. I want to lash out at her and repay her for her harshness
towards me. I've an image of Mary smiling joyously. She thinks
she's with child. But it isn't to be. I have a thought that she
wouldn't gloat so much if she knew that her husband doesn't think
much of her. She loves him but he's not interested in her - it's just
a political alliance. He's not around much, he travels and I hear that
when he's away he takes mistresses.
I'm seeing her now laid in state. Her face is white - she doesn't look
peaceful, just bereft."*
SB: "How do you feel?"
"Numb. I feel I should mourn as she's my sister but emotions won't

come. I feel some sadness but I'm locking it all in. I wear a sombre face as I'm expected to. I turn away from her but I don't look back. I hold my head up high and walk away. I'm conscious that people are looking at me for my reaction.

I'm now remembering us both as young girls, laughing, running and dancing. I'm about 6 or 7. We're outside, near some trees. She's holding something, like a little basket and she's wearing brown again and her hair is covered by a little headdress. We're running to and fro and I can hear her laughing. It's a sweet sound. She didn't laugh like that when we were older. I feel that I love her at this early time in our lives. I'm wondering what happened to her and I regret the loss of the person I used to laugh with. I feel sad, I don't understand what changed. I feel I'm remembering this as an adult, looking back on things.

Things change between us when she was given the throne, when we were old enough to understand what happened to our mothers. I feel as if we were passed around by our father's wives who had their own opinions. Something changed when Mary became accepted as legitimate and I was a bastard. She's acting on that somehow, becoming bitter. I can't understand why she changed, but I feel she changed quickly. I've a vague image of her wedding and a sense of trepidation, worried what she'll do now that she has a husband. It's like the power goes to her head. She's upholding her mother's principles but she's obsessed. She's such a fervent Catholic and I have images of people being burned in fires. The air's thick with smoke. I see wood piled up high around huge stakes and 3 people tied to them, with others watching. It's very distasteful to me, my pious sister murdering people. There's fear - those people believe the same things that I do. I feel revulsion and shame that my kin ordered this.

I'm seeing large crowds now, watching us progress through the streets. It's for Mary but I'm with her, walking slightly behind her. There's a little bit of the old feeling of when we got along but there's reserve on my part - she's Queen and I'm not. She looks over her shoulder at me and smiles hesitatingly. I smile back but I know *things have changed. People are cheering. It feels like one of the last times we're together, like it's the end of how things were. I feel I'm resigning myself to this change."*

Throughout the above Lisa could feel the emotional pain of an older Elizabeth looking back with regret and her voice was hushed and quivering as she shared the Queen's sadness at what might have been. It has to be said that all of the above actually did take place, so once again Lisa had provided details which only a student of history would know.

Little did I know as I listened to all this that in a matter of weeks I would also be regressing another client back into a past life which appeared to have been Mary's, a strange turn of affairs which led to a meeting of Elizabeth and Mary 400 years after they had lived! More on that in the section of the book relating to Mary.

Chapter 8

Liz n'Dud

I'd like to move back now to share with you some more memories Lisa experienced of the intense love affair that Elizabeth had with Robert Dudley, Earl of Leicester. As you probably know this has fascinated historians in the centuries since Elizabeth lived, with many questions about its true nature never really being satisfactorily answered. It may be that Lisa's regressions back into Elizabeth's life can shed some light on the truth. Please remember that Lisa had very little knowledge of Elizabethan history prior to our sessions starting and despite being fascinated by the information we were unearthing she acceded to my request that at no time would she start researching the history books in order to prove the truth of the memories she was reliving. I was obviously fearful that if she did so then there would be a real chance of her confabulating memories, in other words creating memories based on what she had read. This would, of course, have blown apart my search for true, spontaneous past life memories coming solely from Lisa's subconscious. Lisa has given her word that at no time did she delve into any books on Elizabeth and I am convinced that everything that she experienced in trance was her reliving a previous life as Queen Elizabeth.

Robert Dudley appeared many times in our sessions and was like a motif running through the memories of Elizabeth's life that Lisa experienced. She worked through scenes in which Elizabeth's love for him shone through, including intimate moments of tender love as well as at least one of their sexual episodes. Her passion for him shines through, as does her distress over being unable to marry him and her agony over his death. I think we have also confirmed one of the hidden secrets of their relationship.

The memories of their earlier times together have an intensity and a youthful energy which gives Elizabeth a sense of humanity and open-heartedness which she later lost as a result of the burdens of state. She behaves in them just like any young woman in love would do, with spontaneity and an enjoyment of the physicality of it all. One of Lisa's memories epitomise this:

"Someone's holding me by the waist of my dress. I'm indoors. My hair's loose on my shoulders and I'm laughing. It's Robert, and I've been waiting for him. He lifts me up in his arms and I'm looking down at his face, laughing with my hair in his eyes. He sets me down and pushes me to the floor. He's looking down at me. He looks so serious. He's dusty, he's been riding. He kneels down and straddles my knees. He kisses me. I squeal with laughter - dust from the road's all over my face. I feel his cheek against mine and his kiss is hungry and passionate. His hands start to roam. I look at him in mock surprise and tease him about what he's trying to do. But all the while he looks serious, I'm trying to work out why. His hair is all dark and tousled."

It has to be remembered, though, that initially Dudley was trapped in a loveless marriage to Amy, a woman he rarely visited once his affair with Elizabeth was underway, but who remained an obstacle to their relationship.

"I'm in my bedchamber, standing in front of a long mirror, finishing dressing. I feel the farthingale and the bodice. It's only just gone on so the boning is cold and stiff. My hair is loose and long. Behind the mirror is a tall, thin window, diamond-leaded, with rolling grounds and trees outside. I'm in my late teens or early twenties. I have a sense of not wanting to be caught out. His hands are on the back of my neck and he's running my hair through his fingers. It's nice. He kisses the back of my neck and I giggle. He's murmuring 'Bess, my

love Bess' and kissing my neck and shoulders. He runs his hands down to my waist and holds me. He turns me round and runs his hand down my cheek. I smile and feel content - I can be me around him. He leads me to the bed and we sit close with our heads touching. We're not saying much, just smiling. His voice is like a growl when he murmurs. I start to speak but he stops me with a kiss and touches his nose to mine. He's saying goodbye. He has to go away, to visit home. It's a duty, his wife wants his attention. I have to let him go as I can't stand in the way of it. I feel irritated. He gets up and as he leaves he bows down low, giving me a wonderful, warm smile as he flashes his mischievous eyes at me.

Outside is a long corridor with other rooms off. I want to say Nonesuch, something father built on a whim. I can see complicated chimneys and elaborate brickwork, and I think it's near the river."

The death of his wife Amy in 1559 was a convenient one for both Dudley and Elizabeth and rumours abounded at the time that she had been poisoned, but there can be little doubt that her death allowed them to be freer in their relationship.

Their love for each other and the joy which he brought to the young Queen was plain to see when Lisa remembered their times together, her face usually wearing a smile and her voice displaying a soft tenderness as she recounted the pleasure of being in love:-

"I'm in a small room with fewer than 10 people in it. I'm sitting raised up in a high back chair on a single step platform, wearing a cream-coloured dress decorated with gold. It has little panels with flowers embroidered in them."

SB: "How do you feel?"

"Positive, amused. It's an important occasion. Lord Burghley is to my left looking frustrated and agitated. I'm trying hard not to laugh as Robert Dudley is down on one knee, wearing a cape with gold braid on it draped around one shoulder. He's just doffed his little hat

with a feather on it. He's flirting because he knows I can't respond to him. I've conferred a title on him. People to my right are talking, and whilst they are, I tickle the back of his neck. He sits close to me. I think some of those present are foreign, and one is an ambassador. I'm not concentrating though, as I'm too busy looking at Robert as he smiles at me and I'm blushing a little."

This granting of a title upon Dudley might be the occasion in April 1559 when Elizabeth bestowed the Order of the Garter upon him. After a short pause, she continued:

"I'm outside now and it's the afternoon. I'm by the river in London, possibly at Greenwich Palace, walking with Robert. It's quite warm and I'm not wearing anything over my gown, and he's simply in his doublet. There's no-one else around and we're holding hands, smiling, laughing and flirting. He's lifting my hand up and looking deeply into my eyes as he kisses it. His lips are so soft and gentle. I feel all tingly. He's got such a strong gaze, as if he's looking deep inside me. I know he sees who I truly am, if I were free to be. I feel this is after his wife's died, which is why I'm allowing him to be more open. But I always feel he has an agenda, as if he doesn't just want me, he wants to be king. That takes something away from it, but I know that he's not trying to use me just to get somewhere. I know I'd look like a puppet if I married him. Perhaps this is what Lord Burghley sees.

We're in a garden, outside the palace by the river. There are lots of pretty, scented flowers. I've had to share him with his wife which is a little humiliating for me. I don't have to share anyone as I'm Queen. If I were to marry, I would only marry for love, not for an alliance or the desires of Parliament. But I cannot have the man I want so I shall never marry. I feel resigned to it but it makes me feel sad and lonely. I cannot allow him close enough to marry me because of the crown on my head. It doesn't stop me wanting him, lying awake thinking about him or seeking his help when I have a decision to make.

I can see parchment and ink and quills. I'm thinking of the number of times I've written to him. I have to enjoy every moment I am granted to be alone with him."

Lisa paused at this point, sighing and with a degree of melancholy in her voice, so I took the opportunity to ask a question which I felt needed answering in a definitive way. The subject of sex had raised its beautiful head a few times during the regression sessions, with Lisa appearing to imply that Elizabeth and Dudley had gone past 'first base' sometimes, but never really being more specific. I asked her to become more aware of whether or not they had ever enjoyed sexual relations. What happened surprised me.

"It doesn't happen often anymore. It used to happen more frequently before I became Queen, when I'd entertain him. We'd take advantage of hunting parties and accidentally become separated from the group. The closer I became to being Queen there were too many people watching. I was fortunate to have loyal ladies-in-waiting. I have been labelled 'The Virgin Queen' but it is not true."

Lisa paused for a few moments and then I watched as her body softened as she lay in the chair and a broad smile came over her face.

SB: "What's happening now?"

"We're indoors...an encounter with Lord Robert."

At this point Lisa again became silent, before she became completely engrossed in the experience and started to giggle. I watched in amazement as she began to breathe more and more heavily and her hands began clawing the arm of the chair. I realised that she was actually re-experiencing making love with Dudley! Her breathing became louder and she began to arch her body, pushing her head back into the chair as she moaned sensuously. Her breathing, moaning and the physical movements of her body continued for some time before she finally climaxed and with a final sigh and a shudder she relaxed again into a deep trance state, albeit with a flush on her features and a smile on her face. I had actually witnessed a 400 year old royal orgasm! Feeling something of a voyeur I resisted the temptation to say "How was it for you?" and offer her a cigarette, so when she had calmed down I asked Lisa if there was anything else of significance she remembered about that memory. She replied:

"We're in a private room off the corridor, isolated from the rest of the building. He curled his arm round my neck when we were making love."
SB: "Have there been any other lovers?"
"Not in the full sense. There have been other men I've been close to and to a lesser extent intimate with, but not like Robert. Devereux is one - beautiful long legs but a traitor. Robert and I share a depth of passion which I never felt with any other man."

Lisa shivered at this point and I asked her what was happening now.

"I'm still with Robert. He's asleep beside me on my left. He's smiling in his sleep. The bedding is white and our hair is all over the place. I feel quite peaceful. I've escaped for a while. It's quiet, the covers have been kicked off the bed and I don't want to move. I felt liberated just for a little while. He has such a strong power over me. He holds me close, I haven't been held that tight since I was tiny. I'm allowed to be a woman when we're like this, I don't have to be a Queen, I can be simply me. Even though he was so strong when he was kissing my neck he was so gentle. Like making love to the ocean, powerful and gentle at the same time. I feel we were able to take our time with this, which is rare. I feel we are at Kenilworth. It's not long after this that he asks me to marry him and that's when I had to shut off and retreat. It's like I shut the door on it so I shut it away."

Our session time was up so I brought Lisa back out of trance, advising her to have a cold shower! Although I felt like an eavesdropper of something intimate and private, Lisa's orgasmic experience certainly amazed me as it was such an unusual thing to happen in a regression (it's only occurred once before with another client who also experienced having sex in a previous life) but it certainly put paid to my previously held belief in the legend of 'The Virgin Queen.'

Chapter 9

The End of the Affair

Elizabeth's dilemma over marriage to Dudley finally came to a head, it appears, when he proposed to her. It is as if the reality of the situation finally hit home to her and the spell was broken. This climactic event came through in one of our sessions, during which Elizabeth's anguish was plain for me to see as Lisa struggled to hold back the tears caused by her breaking heart:

"I'm standing before a fireplace with Robert. I'm in Leicester's buildings at Kenilworth. The fire crackles. Suddenly I'm nervous. Nervous and excited. I've a mind what he's to do. He asks me to marry him. He does not know the pain that that question can bring. I cannot marry him, but oh, how I wish I could. He asks, even though he knows what the answer will be. I say no."

At this point, Lisa began to cry quietly.

"It will change things now. I feel it will put a distance between us. It's a heavy burden indeed. I have to look after my people, yet who will look after me? He kisses my head most gently. As I turn away I bite my lip and know that in that moment it is changed. I walk away and leave him standing by the fireplace. Part of me wants to run and shut myself in my room, but I have to hold my head high as I walk across the courtyard even though I just feel like crumpling up."

Lisa said nothing for some time, simply sitting sobbing as she felt the overwhelming agony of Elizabeth's emotions, knowing that the glorious love affair that had given her life so much joy and meaning would never be the same again. After a while, once she had composed herself, she continued:

"It's a few years later. He is married now, to Lettice. She is handsome. I feel myself straightening up, holding my head high and masking what I feel. I have to rule, I cannot allow this to cloud me. After the proposal we don't see much of each other. I just feel empty and numb. I had to let go of the one thing I hold most dear. I think of him often. This is not his first wife, he was married around the time I came to the throne to Amy. She died. It was suspected we'd had a hand in her death but it was all very innocent." [Again Lisa was correct. Rumours were circulating after his first wife Amy's death that Dudley had had her poisoned].

At this point Lisa relived, in character, all of Elizabeth's imperiousness in a scene when Robert's second wife Lettice turned up at court. Lisa's face was set and her voice hard and full of anger as she gave vent to the rage Elizabeth had not released over the loss of her beloved Robert:

"I'm at court and aware of a lot of people around me. I'm incredibly angry for she is here. She has the affront to appear with a group of followers which is a poor parody of my own. I will not have that. She assumes an air of importance as if she actually counts for something. I will not stand for it in my court. She is Lettice Knollys - she is now Robert Dudley's wife. I spring to my feet and she has not noticed people have gone quiet, she is too busy simpering. Then she looks at me, holds my gaze before she curtseys. Such arrogance - I will not have that" (at this point Lisa was shouting and spitting out the words). *"Her ladies - what right has she to bring a dozen or so in here - she has no right to hold her own court. She looks nervous now. I order her from the court. She looks positively aghast. I will not tolerate such from her. I tell her that I desire not her presence - the court is a place for friends and advisers, of which she cannot count*

herself amongst them. She turns and runs from the court and her
ladies follow.
I find myself biting my tongue and sit down and try to compose
myself, gripping the arms of the chair. Musicians start to play to
create a diversion - I believe they've been made to do so. I feel a sense
of triumph but if I'm honest it was done out of jealousy, and I know
it will provide fodder for the gossips."

Poor Lettice, who really received the full force of the Monarch's
pent-up emotions and who also had a silly name to put up with
as well. Although at the time of the session I felt that this scene
was an unusual thing for Lisa to have remembered, upon
checking through biographies of Elizabeth I found that this
furious public humiliation of Lettice actually did take place (and
how could she have known this?). After Dudley's proposal of
marriage to Elizabeth and her refusal, their relationship cooled
considerably and Leicester, who had been enjoying an affair with
the Queen's cousin Lettice Knollys, secretly married her. When
Elizabeth found out she felt betrayed (I cannot begin to think
how impotent and desperate she must have felt). Later in 1578
Lettice appeared at court richly-dressed with a large number of
servants. Elizabeth was incensed and gave vent to her frustration
regarding Robert by berating Lettice in front of the whole court
and boxing her ears, shouting 'As but one sun lights the East, so
I shall have but one Queen in England'. Lettice fled from court,
not to reappear for several years.

Another intensely painful session for Lisa, in which she wept
bitterly, was one in which she re-lived Elizabeth's feelings upon
learning of Dudley's death:

"I'm alone at night in my bedchamber holding a candle in my right
hand in a little holder. My hair's down and loose and I'm wearing a
heavy, dark blue wrap. I've had a restless night I think as my
bedclothes are strewn about and crumpled. It's very quiet, there's

no-one around. I feel intensely lonely. Something's happened to make me feel like that. I pick up a letter from the table near the bed and open it very gently. I don't want to damage it, it's very precious to me. I pick up a quill and write something on it - 'His Last.' Then I fold it back up into three so that the top and bottom touch. I'm lonely because he's gone. I feel anger tinged with a lot of sadness - it's such an unjust thing. I feel like sweeping everything off the table, making it as empty as I feel. I get up quickly and walk to the door but I don't know where I'm going so I turn back round. I want so much to scream. I look up at the window and see a beautiful crescent moon. I've never felt this alone. I just stand staring out of the window. There's so much I want to let out but I'm numb somehow. The letter was Robert's. I go back to the table and put it in the bottom drawer of a square box with drawers in it, then close the doors on the box. I sit on the edge of the bed" (by this stage Lisa was very emotional*). "It's the first time in a long time I just rest my head on my knees and wrap my arms around them. After a while I crawl back under the covers and curl up, hoping that no-one hears."*

It was reported that after Dudley's death 'she was so grieved that for some days she shut herself in her chamber alone and refused to speak to anyone until the treasurer and other councillors had the door broken open and entered to see her.' This despair was fully felt by Lisa, who later described the experience as 'harrowing.' Again, Lisa was correct when she mentioned the distraught Queen rereading Dudley's final letter to her and putting it in a cabinet. This was indeed found after Elizabeth's death, marked with the words 'His last letter', in a little coffer that she kept next to her bed.

It was reported by Elizabeth's biographer, Camden, that after her self-imposed incarceration she 'either patiently endured or quietly dissembled' her grief, and indeed Elizabeth's feelings of emptiness were realised by Lisa as she remembered the next day, with the Queen going about her royal duties unable to give a hint of the emptiness she was feeling to those around her:

"It's the morning and I'm sat with my ladies around me. Someone's brushing my hair and curling and pinning it. I can feel my feet being put into shoes and someone pulling a ruff around my neck and placing a high collar with it. I'm just letting them do it, staring out across the room. Someone puts a string of pearls around my neck, and I can feel they're cold. I have pearls in my hair as well and one sitting at the front, a drop pearl, hanging on my forehead. I'm wearing a black dress, and the ruff and collar are edged with gold. I stand and the ladies skirt left and right and curtsey. I take a deep breath, try to compose myself and stride across the chamber. People open doors for me and I stride across a wide hall with pillars and a floor of black and white tiles. The men there drop to their knees and take their hats off. At the end of the hall an old man with a grey beard waits for me. He's holding a staff or a stick of some sort. He walks beside me and talks quietly. I'm supposed to listen but I'm not paying much attention. I leave him and turn along a passage into a garden. I sit alone, smelling the plants and the herbs there."

So ended what is surely one of history's most poignant love stories. I honestly feel that Lisa's memories of Elizabeth's and Robert's times together have put flesh and blood on what is often glossed over or dismissed in many history books, bringing a real sense of the passionate nature of their affair. How tragic it was that they were unable to live their lives together as man and wife, a sorrow that the Queen carried to the end of her days.

Famous Past Lives

Chapter 10

A Royal Child?

It's said that many rumours circulated frequently during Elizabeth's life that she had secretly borne children, many of them malicious gossip with no proof to support them. There were also stories about her promiscuity which were also dismissed by the authorities, who obviously played up the image of the Virgin Queen as a matter of state policy. However, there have been frequent assertions regarding her relationship with Robert Dudley, with many people unable to believe that their love was simply platonic, given Elizabeth's notorious flirtatiousness. It does seem hard to believe that she did not enjoy sexual relations with Dudley, especially given the openness towards sex and sexual matters that prevailed in society at that time. Our modern societal view of sex is based on Victorian values which were utterly repressive compared with life in Elizabethan England. If Lisa's experiences as Elizabeth which have been recounted so far are true (and I have to say that I believe that they are) then Elizabeth enjoyed an occasional sex life with him (as well as at least one pleasant orgasm!) which belies her public reputation as a virgin.

Having said that, it was with a real sense of surprise when, during one of our later sessions of regression, Lisa relived something which must make us question whether the Queen really did have a child to Dudley. As usual, she went into trance and I allowed her subconscious to take us into the past life. She began speaking softly and slowly:

"I'm lying in bed and there are people stood around. I feel weak and don't have the strength to speak to them. I can hear my maid's voices

50

coming from either side of me and male voices coming from the end of the bed. Someone's brushed my hair out and it's all over the pillows and my shoulders. I hear a fire crackling. They seem to be concerned. I hear the rustling of someone unfolding a parchment and someone asking me to name a successor. It sounds like Burghley. "Madam you must name someone" he says. He sounds terribly afraid. They think I'm dying. I name Robert Dudley as Protector, should I be taken. I'm aware of audible gasps and then a hush. 'Tis not their preferred person but such is my choice. I can think of no other I would trust.

I'm aware of the lace cuffs on the shift I'm wearing, feeling it on the back of my hands. I feel bloated and uncomfortable. The maids are dressed as if attending childbirth, with white aprons and their hair covered in white caps. They do not leave my side unless relieved by another. The room is dark, the curtains closed, windows shut and the fire always lit. I feel a delirium, things feel remote. I hear a female voice, as if in pain and other hushed voices and things being moved. I feel cold, wet fabric on my brow. The women on either side of me are holding me and propping me up. I feel so removed, as if it's happening to someone else. There's screaming again and I feel pain."

Throughout this Lisa had been becoming increasingly tense, and at this point her breathing came hard through clenched teeth. Her hands pushed down into the chair. Her body really was feeling some of the tension of the birth.

"I'm pushing my hands down very hard into the bed. My hair is stuck to my face. Again I hear the screaming and feel a sense of determination."

Her face was drawn as her breathing came quicker. She started to moan.

"I'm aware of blood. I sink back and my head drops back. Hands are laying me down against the pillars. The room is so hot and stifling. I'm aware of a desire to move my head from side to side as if I'm battling with something. I want to clench my teeth really hard. They're all hushed and purposeful. There are terribly painful sensations in my belly. I push myself up on the pillows. I'm so tired. I hear a child crying. It makes me want to cry. Everything feels so remote, so detached. Someone lays me back down and wipes strands of hair from my cheeks, and lays a coverlet over me. Two ladies, one on either side, are sat down on chairs. I have a desire to sleep."

Lisa lay quietly in the chair for some time, as if exhausted by the rigours of what she'd experienced. After a while I asked her to move on to the next significant part of the memories:

"It's later in the day and I'm sat up in bed wearing a heavy brocade gown. Someone has washed and brushed out my hair. My ladies are waiting for orders from me. I feel drained of emotion - it must be placed aside. He must be taken from this place. Thomas must come for him. One of my ladies is speaking out of turn: 'My lady, the child's father...' I cut across her – 'he must not know. The child must be gone and that's the end of it.' They all curtsey and leave me. I wait till I know they are far enough away and then curl my hands into fists, dig my nails into the palms of my hands as hard as I can."

At this, Lisa began to cry uncontrollably, her face contorted in agony as she sobbed and howled. I had seen her relive some of the Queen's emotions before but not like this. For some time she wept bitterly as she felt all of Elizabeth's grief and anguish. Accustomed as I am as a Therapist to witness people becoming emotional whilst in trance, I have to say I was deeply moved. I knew though that I had to let her go through it so she could release it all from her system.

After some time her emotions began to subside so I asked her to go on. Speaking quietly and in a controlled manner she continued:

"I have to force myself to unclench my hands. I wait until the fire dies in the hearth. Slowly I regain my composure. I'm trying so hard not to think, because if I think of it..." Her voice trailed away as once more she cried, feeling the Queen's distress. *"I have the name Arthur, after my father's brother. I don't think I've ever felt more alone."*

SB: "Let yourself move onto the next significant time."

"It's a long time after. Maybe a year or so later. I'm writing a prayer on a parchment. It's one of those rare moments when I have time to myself. When I think of him I wonder how he is growing. But I can't allow myself to think of it for too long. It's not to be thought of now. I dare not."

SB: "Move on again to the next significant part of these memories."

"One of my ladies is trying to speak of the boy. He's been seen. She's trying to tell me how like his father he is. I'm aware of a ferocious response on my part - I do not want this subject raised - I have long forbidden them to speak of it. It's folly to speak of what cannot be changed...and yet I long to hear. He's a young man now." Lisa sighed and her voiced trembled as it trailed away.

SB: "Is this still painful to you?"

"Always. But it cannot be allowed to rise up and be experienced."

SB: "Move on to a later significant time."

"I have purposely forbidden myself to listen to the whispers that fly around court. I hear tell that he is to go abroad. Part of me aches to think of him leaving, but I must close off to such things. I do not have the luxury of mortal emotion. I do not have time to dwell on it. I am a queen. I have not the right to feel after all." Lisa smiled ironically. *"To do so would be to give in, to lose control and authority. And as hard as it pulls at me and as sharply as it hurts me, I must turn away. I will think of it no longer."*

Lisa came out of trance at this point, as if to emphasise the ending of those memories. As I write this now I am struck again by the pain and suffering which Elizabeth had to endure as a result of her love for Robert Dudley. Unable to marry the man who meant everything to her, ultimately as a result of her position unable to even continue their relationship as lovers, she is then unable to mother their child and bring him up as her own. The child is secreted out of the palace as soon as he is born and then, one assumes, he is raised by others at a big enough distance from the Queen not to be connected to her in any way. How must she have felt living her life with all that suffering inside her? I doubt she ever healed her broken heart.

What I find amazing, though, is the fact that Lisa came up with the birth of a boy to Elizabeth, something which was often rumoured during her lifetime but usually dismissed by historians as rumours which were intended to discredit her by her enemies and detractors. I would guess that most people, like Lisa, who had not studied the period or Elizabeth's life, would probably think of her as the Virgin Queen because this is the image of Elizabeth that has been strongly handed down to us by posterity. However, when I began researching the life of Elizabeth to try and corroborate Lisa's past life experiences, I was stunned to find that there is a little-known story which may confirm Lisa's memories concerning the birth of an illegitimate child to Elizabeth and Dudley called Arthur. The story, a shortened version of which is as follows, does have a strong ring of authenticity.

In June 1587 a young Englishman was held by the Spanish authorities and suspected of being a spy. Either his ship had ran aground or the ship in which he was travelling was intercepted by a Spanish patrol (I've read two different accounts of how he ended up in Spain) but he claimed that he had become a Catholic and was on a pilgrimage via Spain to France. He was imprisoned at San Sebastian and after a few days was taken to see an English

Roman Catholic exile living in Madrid, Sir Francis Englefield, who committed his 'confession' to paper. The story the young man (he was aged around 25) told was an incredible one, claiming to be the bastard son of Elizabeth and Dudley.

He said his name was Arthur Dudley (Lisa was correct with the name) and he had been brought up as a small child in a village some 60 miles from London with several other children whom he thought were his siblings, by Robert Southern, whom he always believed was his father. Southern was a servant of Queen Elizabeth's former governess Katherine Ashley. When Arthur was about 5, Southern took him to London and placed him (but not his brothers or sisters) in the care of Katherine Ashley's husband, John. He was given a gentleman's education but as he grew up was barred from travelling abroad, so he ran away intending to travel to Spain. He was caught and shown an order which had come from the Privy Council commanding that he be prevented at all costs from leaving the country. Eventually, however, he was allowed to enlist as a volunteer to fight in the Netherlands, and in 1580 travelled to Ostend.

Towards the end of 1583 he received a message asking him to return to England at once as his father was very ill and wished to tell him something of importance before he died. He found Southern dying at Evesham, but before he died he confessed the truth of Arthur's upbringing in front of a witness, a local school-master. Southern told him that he was not his real father, but that one day he had been ordered by Katherine Ashley to go to Hampton Court where he was given a newborn baby by one of the Queen's ladies-in-waiting. He was told that the baby was the illegitimate son of one of the ladies at court who would be ruined if the Queen found out about her misconduct, and he was ordered to bring up the child as his own son. Southern told Arthur that he was this child, and that it was Ashley who had paid for his education. At first, when Arthur asked Southern who his father was the dying man refused to say, but finally he told him the truth, that he was the illegitimate child of Elizabeth and Dudley.

That is the bare bones of the story, around which there are other strong pieces of circumstantial evidence, to suggest that Arthur was indeed who he says he was. Dr Paul Doherty, who has written a book detailing what he considers to be the truth about Arthur Dudley being Elizabeth's child, has unearthed various pieces of information which seem to bear out his claim. One of these is a letter in the British Library dated May 28th, 1588 from an English spy to his bosses in London in which he describes the interrogation of Arthur Dudley in Spain and hints that the Spanish authorities took his claim seriously, to the extent of housing him at the Spanish court and granting him a pension. The spy also stated that Arthur Dudley bore more than a passing resemblance to his father Robert Dudley, the Earl of Leicester. Could it be that when Elizabeth was confined to bed in 1561 (at the time when her love affair with Dudley was at its height) with a mysterious illness she was in fact pregnant? According to witnesses she was suffering from dropsy (now known as oedema), an abnormal swelling of the body due to a build-up of fluid. The Spanish ambassador reported that she had a swelling of the abdomen, and it does seem highly likely, now that we have seen the extent of the passion between the two, that she could have been carrying Dudley's child. I am astonished that Lisa experienced this (until recently) little-known footnote to the life of Elizabeth, something which she would not have known had she not been truly reliving the life of the Queen in our sessions.

Something else which struck me as unusual in the session was Lisa's claim that during this crisis, when it was feared the Queen might die, that she named her lover Robert Dudley as successor to the throne. I felt that this was highly unlikely as Dudley was not of royal stock, but once more when I checked the history books I was surprised to find that this did actually take place. It is reported that in October 1562 (when she was 29 years old)

Queen Elizabeth was at Hampton Court when she fell danger-
ously ill and was diagnosed as having smallpox. Her life hung in
the balance and as her councillors gathered round her bedside,
anxious to make provision for the country's governance should
she die, she ordered them to make Robert Dudley Lord Protector
of England. Could it be that Lisa was confusing this time in
Elizabeth's life with the birth of a child a year or so earlier? Or,
had Elizabeth on both occasions demanded that Dudley be
appointed as Protector? Either way, I think the very fact that she
came up with this at all in our session was quite remarkable.

Chapter 11

Looking Back on a Life

Our final session of regression together was one in which we tied up a few loose ends and took Lisa through some of Elizabeth's later memories as well as her death. We had completed quite a number of sessions by this time and I felt that we had covered many aspects of Elizabeth's life, enough to give a strong impression of her as a human being rather than just a royal character from history. Also, Lisa was finding it difficult to devote time to the sessions. Besides this her curiosity and desire to start studying Elizabeth's life in order to see if her experiences in hypnosis were indeed factual, played a part in our decision to have one last session and then close the book, as it were, on the memories.

Elizabeth's last thoughts as she lay dying, as we shall see, were of Robert and a desire to be reunited with him after death. Before that though, as she lay on her deathbed, the ailing Queen's mind went back to another man who was reputed to have been one of her lovers:

"Old age brings tiredness and despair. What I'd lost. What price my duty? They marvelled at why I'd shout at times but they had no idea the pressure, the responsibility, the constant threat. I keep seeing people's faces in my mind's eye. There's a man much younger than I. He is Robert Devereux, Earl of Essex."

Lisa then appeared to slip back a few years to when Elizabeth and Devereux had been close. She was in her mid-fifties, he over thirty years her junior.

"There is a strong affection between us, a genuine one on my part, but I have a sense that he conspires against me. He is plotting, and there are a good many of them seeking my power. He is to be executed for treason. I feel humiliated that once again I am betrayed by one I have given affection to. He is a handsome man, with beautiful thick hair and expressive eyes. The ladies at court choose to look upon him when they think I see them not. There are those who think it inappropriate that one as old as I should choose to court one as young as he. But I think age matters not. I think of how different things would have been if I had been allowed to be with my Robin. I could have given them a king in him, but I knew it could never happen. He loved me before there was any question of my becoming Queen - it was not just about my title. I sense a visit I made to Kenilworth and Robert nearly bankrupted himself enter-taining on that scale, I think for about 19 days. He was trying to get my attention, which had he looked inside his heart he would have known all along he had. It troubles me that we were never able to have what we both wanted."

Once more Lisa was correct with this, as in the summer of 1575 Elizabeth went on a 'royal progress' which culminated in Dudley providing the most costly and extravagant entertainments of her reign at Kenilworth, although it lasted for 10 days and not 19. These included banquets, pageants, hunting, dancing, bear-baiting, fireworks and a richly costumed mythological masque. Everything was on a lavish scale at an incredible cost, from which (as Lisa rightly stated) Leicester's purse never recovered. She was also correct in knowing that the true purpose of it all was to convince Elizabeth to marry him, but it was an oppor-tunity which failed and which would never come his way again. It is said that after Kenilworth he pursued her with less ardour and began looking elsewhere for love.

"I feel old and with a sense of weariness I recall Devereux again. I find it difficult to be passionate as I was when I was younger. I grow weary of scandals and struggles and those who seek to undermine."

Lisa sighed deeply and was silent for some time. It was as if the act of recollecting was becoming harder. Finally she spoke, but at this point Lisa began speaking forcefully and for the final time I witnessed her taking on the personality of the Queen, the tone of her voice and her demeanour becoming regal and vehement:

"I'm older again, looking back, in my bed. I remember the day I had to send Devereux to his death. The young fool. Tried to rise in the streets against me and for that he laid his pretty neck on the block. It's the privilege of the Queen to take the lives of traitors. It's not a privilege I hold dear, especially taking the lives of those I loved and my family. Devereux made me feel foolish. Foolish for wasting time and affection on him. He reminded me of someone else. He hurt me when he turned and I had little hesitation signing his warrant. I would not be made a fool of in my own kingdom. When that anger subsided though I felt tired. They saw me as a woman, yet I am the daughter of Henry. Those such as Devereux who stand in my way will be put down, but what people don't see is that I have to live with the consequences. I shed tears when he was gone. Tears of anger and rage."

After a pause she quietened again and her voice softened:

"With Devereux's death another part of my spirit was extinguished and with his passing I miss my Robin all the more."
SB: "Tell me more about your relationship with Devereux".
"We spent many hours sitting closely together, he holding my hands and kissing my fingers. He'd talk of my beauty and read poetry to me. He tried to impress. He was at my side at State functions, banquets and balls, and I knew people were laughing. He was a little

amusement for me. He reminded me of Robin. I sought so hard to fill the void that Robin left, but no-one could do that. Having Robin with me was the closest thing I have ever done. I did not take the boy into my bed. He was attracted to my power, not my old and ravaged body. My cousin paraded the boy before me and I was aware of her motivation, but in his eyes I saw someone else. I would say there was a strong chance he was Robin's son. He was the last time that I would have someone at my side. It was but a trifle, a fancy. There was no substance to what I shared with Robert Devereux but it made me feel less old for a time.

Robert Dudley left such a void that I changed greatly after him. I retreated into myself and became more aloof. I became remote in my manner and the pain caused bitterness in me. That, coupled with the pressure and barrage of responsibility left me tired. I lost some of my energy when he left. It would have caused an uproar if I'd made him my husband, and there was the small question of his marriage. It left me tired and weak, and I felt no true happiness or joy." She sighed and went quiet. *"Enough now."*

Lisa's face became serious for a time, and she breathed heavily, as if life was ebbing out of her. She was silent for a while, before a soft smile lit up her face and she began to speak in a whisper, her voice faltering:

"I see trees, an orchard, apples. He is with me - Robert's there. He turns me in his hands and we run together. We're young again. I hear him laughing and see the colour of his face. I smile at him. Our horses are tethered to the trees. I wear green and he jokes that I'll blend in with the trees and he'll have to search all the harder for me. There's so much laughter. I see blue skies…"

Her voice trailed away and she let out a low sigh. Lisa lay in silence for a few minutes, before she continued in her own voice:

"I think this is the last thing I remembered as I'm dying. I just drifted off as I saw us together. It was such a welcome sleep. Such a wonderful feeling - the weight of 70 years just gone."

SB: "Let yourself experience leaving the body and moving into Spirit"

"I feel myself being pulled gently away, with hands on my arms and shoulders. The hands guide me, I'm floating. Once again I'm young with long thick hair and a pretty dress and I can laugh. I see faces all around, hundreds and thousands of faces, welcoming me. And there he is, just as of old. He pulls me to him and holds me tight. I feel that I've come home." Lisa began to cry. *"I feel sadness and joy. It's all done and I'm free. I look down and can see people standing around my body, with someone trying to prise the ring off my finger. I hear my maids crying but I don't feel anything as I look at it. It's over."*

And so it was. Lisa's last words ended a fascinating journey for us both. Queen Elizabeth I died on 24th March 1603. There seemed to be a completeness in that both she and her true love, Robert Dudley, Earl of Leicester, were finally together at last.

POSTSCRIPT

Some time after Lisa and I had finished our sessions together and as I was gathering together my notes for this book, I asked Lisa if she could give me her impressions of the regressions and how she has integrated the knowledge that she is the reincarnation of Elizabeth I into her life. This is what she wrote:

I have to say that before I started my regression sessions with Steve, I hadn't given any thought to the concept of past lives, except possibly as interesting things that happened to other people and occasionally got written about in magazines! I am not a delusional person or prone to imagining things and I started the sessions with Steve because I was looking for answers – strange things – pictures and so on were spontaneously popping into my head and I honestly thought I might be going mad and I wanted to find out what was going on.

I got a lot more than I bargained for! We worked together on my past life for a couple of years and it turned out to be the most fantastic and interesting journey that I had never intended or expected to go on in my life! It felt like reading a book that you can't bear to put down because you just have to know what's going to happen next. Often I was confused, because I didn't understand how or why this was happening to me and always amazed at the things I was saying and experiencing – not least of all when it became obvious who I had apparently been. I was sceptical at first - after all, how many others have claimed to have famous former personas - I felt so many emotions and recalled wonderful things, everything was so vivid, like turning a kaleidoscope and being given a wonderful new pattern each time. I admit to still being a tiny bit sceptical – but that's just about questioning my experiences and staying rational, balanced and reasoned about life.

The regression has had an impact on my life. I learned a lot about myself along the way. I realise that certain things about me seemed to be parallel to how I was in my past life. Little things I did, had been interested in, drawn to and so on actually seem to make sense. Because I was looking back at a former personality, I started, probably subconsciously at first, to look more closely at who I am in the present. Not only did I have a fantastic time exploring an unexpected curveball thrown at me by life, but I ended up understanding myself better, and I think that's a really positive conclusion to my work with Steve. I'm glad I decided to dive in and explore my mind, and the whole experience has opened me up to new possibilities.

Chapter 12

Another Queen Unveiled

Kate came to me for help with a variety of issues, including suffering from stress and anxiety and having a weight problem. A retired staff nurse aged 41, she had been forced to leave work due to a head injury sustained in an accident. She was lively and fun to talk to but it was obvious that her jovial façade was a mask, hiding a wealth of painful feelings inside her. Her overeating was a way for her to anaesthetise the negative emotions she was carrying, negative emotions which stemmed from a dysfunctional, emotionally difficult childhood and (her subconscious indicated) from several past lives.

As usual when working in regression therapy we spent some sessions opening up childhood memories in order to release the locked-in emotions they contained and to heal Kate's 'Inner Child'. We also began exploring some of her previous lives which were causing the problems. At this stage nothing of note came through in our therapy together and there was no hint that Kate's therapy process would be anything other than a standard process.

Although Kate went quite easily into trance she was not very 'visual' in that she didn't see her past life experiences vividly. She felt them (physically and emotionally) and she could get an intuitive understanding of what was happening in them but when she saw the past life events in her mind's eye it was like seeing them through a thin veil. Unlike my sessions with Lisa who saw everything very clearly and distinctly, Kate's past life experiences were a little bit more vague and subsequently harder to get into to open them up. This did lead to some initial confusion when she began reliving the memories which are the subject of this book.

After a few sessions Kate shared with me a couple of what she called "obsessions", one of which would prove to be particularly significant. She told me that she had always been obsessed with Lancaster bombers, and secondly with Tudor times and Queen Elizabeth. She also had recurring dreams of being a man in some form of warfare, and she had two main fears in life: fear of flying and fear of fire. In one of our regression sessions she experienced the reasons for the recurring dreams as well as the cause of her fears of flying and fire, as she re-lived a past life as an airman in a WWII bomber which is hit by enemy fire:

> "I'm on a plane, I can hear it shuddering and stuttering. I'm shouting frantically "Get out, get out." There's a fire on the plane. I feel so frightened. Somebody's saying "We're going down Skipper". I don't want to die, I don't want to die."

Kate became very emotional and anxious, breathing quickly and most of her words were incomprehensible as she cried and shook with terror. Finally, she let out a long sigh and laid in the therapy chair in silence.

SB: "What are you aware of now?"

"Whiteness, peace. It's over."

That's a fairly typical past life experience and I include it here as an aside not because it's relevant to the theme of famous past lives, but because it highlights how many of our fears and phobias come from past life traumas. Kate's re-experiencing of that death helped to reduce both of her fears and the frequency of her recurring dreams.

Her mentioning of her obsession with Tudor times also made me wonder if it was related to a previous life, so in our next session I regressed her back to see if we could connect to the cause of her fascination with that period of history. It was here that things began to get interesting!

SB: "Whereabouts are you?"

"I'm outside somewhere. It feels as if I'm in the grounds of a palace, somewhere like Hampton Court. It's a sunny day"

SB: What's happening? Are you a man, a woman, a girl, a boy or something else?"

"I'm a young woman, watching some young children laughing and playing outside on the grass. I don't feel as if they're my children - I think it's my position to look after them. The little girl closest to me is laughing the most. She's wearing a green dress and she has deep ginger hair. I can hear myself saying 'don't do that' as though I'm telling someone off. I pick the little girl up and spin her around. The words 'what are you doing my pretty maid' keep coming into my mind. I feel happy." After a brief pause, she continued:

"I'm older now and the same girl's grown up - she's maybe 16 or 17. She's sitting with a mirror in front of her and I'm brushing her hair. It's really long and golden-coloured. She seems special and pretty.

I've moved to another scene now. The girl seems lonely and unloved. She's sad, sitting in the window-sill on a nice square cushion with her feet up. I ask her if she's alright and she taps the cushion and asks me to come and talk to her.

I see her now standing in the sunshine smelling a flower. She is so beautiful. I feel privileged to look after her."

These glimpses of a Tudor life, in a regal setting with a young woman with long red hair, understandably rang a few bells with me as at this time I had completed several sessions with Lisa. I asked Kate if she could become more aware of the beautiful young girl.

"I feel like I'm making it up, but I get the name Elizabeth."

After a pause, Kate stiffened and became tense.

"I'm in a heavy dress, bustling down a stark, grey stone corridor with windows. I'm cross because I can't find her. There's a lot of commotion - there are men on horseback. What do they want? I'm

really upset and shouting 'please don't hurt her.' They're taking the girl away that I look after. I'm scared, angry and helpless. She's shouting 'help me' but I can't as there are too many of them. I feel like she's being ripped away from me - I feel so sad and frightened. I can't help my beautiful, beautiful girl. I'm worried that they're going to take her away and kill her. I'm tugging someone's garment and saying 'please don't take her away.' There's absolute mayhem."

After a few seconds Kate sighed and relaxed again, and as our session was nearly over I asked her to let go of the visions which she'd been seeing, but before I brought her out of trance I used a hypnotic technique known as an Ideo-Motor Response which allows her subconscious to take control of a finger and to use the finger to signal 'yes' to any of my questions by raising the finger. I asked her subconscious mind if the girl in the past life memories was called Elizabeth, to which the finger raised to signal 'yes.' I then asked her subconscious if this was the same Elizabeth who would later become Queen of England. Again, her subconscious replied with a 'yes.'

We were both intrigued by this turn of events, and we began trying to work out just who Kate had been in that lifetime, and her relationship to the future Queen Elizabeth I. The most likely explanation, given that she seemed to be looking after Elizabeth and that she had some sense of responsibility towards her, was that she was a governess or lady-in-waiting. However, we were unable to come to a firm conclusion so we agreed to do further work in future sessions to see if we could uncover more details as to Kate's identity in the past life that we had opened up. In the meantime, I asked her not to read any books or study in any way anything relating to Elizabeth or Tudor times, which she readily agreed to.

Chapter 13

The Penny Drops

In our next session, once Kate was in trance, her subconscious initially took her into a different past life which we had worked upon in a previous hypnotherapy session. Once we had done this we had a bit of time left in which to explore the Tudor life again. After a pause as she moved from one previous life to another, a smile came over her face as she recounted a pleasant scene:

> "Somebody is shouting 'Mary, where are you?' There are children there. She's got a beautiful green and golden dress on and she has ginger hair. She's about 7 years of age. The little boy's younger, about 5. I must be in my late teens. We're holding hands and dancing in a circle and laughing. I feel so close to her, she could be mine. I like spoiling Elizabeth and combing her hair. A woman calls us. I feel really happy."

Kate was, however, from this brief glimpse, unable to get a sense of her identity and so we finished the session. We were both working on the assumption the she was probably a governess to Elizabeth, and we wondered if she had been called Mary as this was the name that had come through to Kate whilst in trance. In an effort to see if we could trigger any further memories, I explained that I happened to be working at that time with a woman who appeared to have been Elizabeth in her past life and I wondered if Kate would be interested in meeting up with her. I was also genuinely curious as to what would happen when two people who had been together in a past life met up for the first time in this lifetime. Kate readily agreed, as did Lisa when I contacted her, so I arranged that the 3 of us would get together a few days later. They also both agreed to do a joint regression.

What happened at that meeting was not what I was expecting. I was hoping that upon being introduced to each other Lisa and Kate would immediately recognise each other in some way as Kate appeared to have had a real closeness and love for Elizabeth in her past life sessions. I wondered if they would even feel a strong bond of affection without knowing why. I was also hoping that we would get clues as to the identity of Elizabeth's governess.

Quite the opposite occurred however. I had half expected them to hug and act like long-lost friends but upon first meeting each other Lisa and Kate recoiled and became quite distant, with Lisa's bearing becoming somewhat haughty. They shook hands coldly and the atmosphere between them seemed chilly and uncomfortable. This took me by surprise.

We talked about their regression experiences and how we wondered if Kate could have been Elizabeth's governess, but the atmosphere between them as they shared their experiences in our sessions was frosty and they both seemed uncomfortable with the situation. It was with a sense of relief that I took them both into trance together and as Lisa was the most visual of the two (in that she could see her past life events quite clearly in her mind's eye) most of the information came from her:

L: "I'm indoors. It's daytime. The sun's streaming through a window. I'm standing with a lady in front of me. She's a few inches taller than me and she has a round face and a kind expression and brown eyes. I'm about 10 and she's about 30. She knows me well, better than my family. She gives me a reassuring smile and I feel safe and comforted. I want to call her Kat. Now I've moved to another memory. She's helping me to dress for an occasion. I'm in my early teens and she's helping me to fasten a collar and ruff. We're trimming the outfit with other people fetching and carrying. There's a four-poster bed to the right of us. It's fairly important *occasion and I'm taking a lot of time and effort. The dress is a dark colour."*

Kate's experience was not as detailed, but she did appear to relive part of the same scene:

K: "I feel there's a lot of bustling as we're getting ready and people are scooping up clothes to put away. I don't want to put on the red dress."

Lisa then moved to one of Elizabeth's most horrific memories, that of being taken to the Tower of London. This surprised me at the time, as so far both Lisa and Kate appeared to have been experiencing happy times together.

L: "I'm on the top of the steps at Traitor's Gate, my dress trailing in the water. Kat's gone ahead of me. I won't move and Kat's willing me to cooperate to move away from the steps. The guards are waiting to take us to where I'll be held. I feel I want to be stubborn and tell them it isn't right. I look at Kat - she looks worried and she doesn't want me to upset them. We're surrounded by guards, some holding pikes. We walk across a courtyard and down a dark passage through a heavy metal door. It shuts behind us with a hard, cold clang."

Throughout the regressions Kate relived a few memories but nothing of any real importance, so we finished the session without us getting any further knowledge regarding the possibility of Kate being the young Princess Elizabeth's governess Katherine (or Kat as Elizabeth seems to have called her). After a somewhat stilted hug between Kate and Lisa we said our goodbyes and went our separate ways.

The next day Kate emailed me with her impressions, and the penny dropped for both of us. She wrote:

Hi Steve

I thought I'd send my thoughts and feelings now before I forget. It was a different meeting than I had expected with Lisa. I did not recognise her when I came into the room, but when she stood up with her shoulders back that reminded me of Elizabeth. When we held hands it was like someone walking over my grave, I went cold to the core with shivers up my legs and spine. I did not feel the warm rush of instant love I thought I might get when meeting her. During the regression I did not see Elizabeth at all but felt the feelings of some of the situations or (perhaps) similar situations. I came home deflated - I knew I was not the nursemaid to Queen Elizabeth. I phoned my friend Jane who is a Tudor expert (bear in mind that as you requested I have not read any books on Elizabeth) and she explained to me that Elizabeth's older sister Mary helped to look after the young Elizabeth, putting onto her all her maternal feelings. Mary spoiled Elizabeth with presents etc. and eventually whilst still young Elizabeth was moved away to other households.

I don't wish to sound presumptuous but was I Mary who became Mary I (Bloody Mary)?

Of course, this made so much sense and fitted in totally with Kate's past life memories. I was shocked - had I really come upon the reincarnations of both Queen Elizabeth and Queen Mary? Had I introduced them to each other after a gap of over 400 years? This would also explain why Lisa had initially remembered a happy memory of her governess Katherine (or Kat) Ashley as we had focussed on Kate being the reincarnation of her at the start of our meeting, before she relived being sent to the Tower by Mary. We know that this had seriously traumatised Elizabeth and was possibly something she never fully recovered from and for which she could not forgive Mary. Meeting again the perpetrator of that trauma in this life obviously triggered Lisa to spontaneously regress to it. No wonder Lisa and Kate had been so frosty with each other!

Chapter 14

Visions of Mary

In our next hypnotherapy session together Kate and I worked with the 'possibility' that she could have been Mary Tudor, but with my scepticism firmly in place I was determined not to lead Kate into any falsely implanted memories in any way. If she truly was the reincarnation of Mary then the information had to come from her subconscious mind whilst she was in trance and not from me.

Once she was in trance I guided her back to the Tudor past life. She immediately began to feel very tense and her body stiffened as she lay in the chair.

"I'm feeling more and more uptight, and I want to clench my teeth - my shoulders feel tense and it's as if I've got period pains."

By itself this may not appear to be very significant, but after I completed all of my sessions with Kate I began to read some biographies of Mary Tudor and it seems that throughout her life Mary suffered from abdominal pains, which brought on symptoms of depression, difficulty in breathing and painful swelling in the abdomen. It's reported that Mary's suffering was profound and regular. Strange that Kate should have experienced this at the beginning of our work uncovering memories of Mary (I've never had anyone else in any Past Life Regression sessions mention such a thing), especially as she'd never read or researched Mary in any way.

Kate continued:

"I'm wearing a good quality, well-fitted dress, with a square neck and ruffs. It's embroidered with a gold pattern on it. I can feel a man's hands on my shoulders and he's shaking me. It's like I've been crying and upset and he's telling me to stop it. He picks me up and spins me round. He's not being nasty, he's trying to bring me round as if I've been hysterical."

One can only speculate as to what was happening here, but could it be that this man was trying to break Mary out of one of her many bouts of pain and panicking due to her illness? I later read in one biography of her that in 1531 the Venetian ambassador to the English court reported that she had been ill for several weeks with 'hysteria.'

After a pause, Kate moved from this unpleasant scene into something gentler, and she began to laugh:

"I'm sitting with the man on a four-poster bed - we're wearing big baggy white nightshirts. It's a huge bed with a big embroidered canopy and embroidered curtains round it. We're sitting talking and eating fruits. I think I'm in my late 20's. I feel that I love him and idolise him. He's dressed now, and he kisses me and leaves the room - I hear the words 'Mary my sweet love'. His name's Philip and he has bright blue eyes - blue like the sky. How I love him.
The thought's just come to me that I'll have to watch the bitch my sister otherwise she'll take him from me. I'll have to ask my fool to keep a close eye on her"

This reference to a 'fool' is interesting, as most English monarchs for centuries had employed jesters to keep their royal courts amused. These jesters, otherwise known as 'innocents' or 'fools', often enjoyed a good deal of power and would sometimes be used as an extra pair of eyes and ears to pick up on any intrigues that may endanger the King or Queen. Mary had two fools at court, firstly Will Somer, who she had inherited from her father

King Henry VIII, and a female fool known simply as Jane. I think it unlikely that such a reference would have been made by Kate if she had just been making all this up!

> *"I've moved to another time now. I'm walking round a formal rose garden in deep thought. If she's plotting against me I'll show her who's boss. The name Leicester's in my head. I want to say that Elizabeth's got a lover but he's already married - she's a little fool. Edward's on the throne but he's not very old. He thinks he's old enough to know what to do but the others are leading him astray.*
>
> *I want to celebrate mass. I'll put it right even if they try to stop me. I think it's something to do with mass. I'm kneeling in front of a priest who's doing the sign of a cross. He's talking in Latin. There are some ladies-in-waiting standing behind me.*
>
> *I'm now sitting in a big wide window-sill reading and looking out of the window. I feel lonely - I'm glad I've got my books. I enjoy reading and studying. I'm in my late 20's, maybe 29-30. I'm thinking 'let Philip come home safe'. I think he's my husband. I feel like he's gone away, he's gone back to Spain. I'm ever so lonely when he's not there. I don't feel I have anyone else to confide in. I can't trust my lady companions and they gossip behind my back. I wish he'd come home. My dress is a rich, dark red."*

The session ended and I felt much more comfortable with the likelihood of Kate being Mary rather than Elizabeth's governess. The information she'd come up with all fitted in totally with what I'd learnt about Elizabeth's and Mary's lives as a result of my previous hypnosis sessions with Lisa. Mary was indeed a practising Catholic who later attempted to reintroduce Catholicism as England's national faith. Mary had indeed fallen in love with King Philip II of Spain, a relationship which appeared to have been extremely one-sided. Philip spent much of his time away from Mary and there were constant rumours at the time about his marital infidelities, including rumours of his attraction to the young Princess Elizabeth. Mary's jealousy was well-known, as was Elizabeth's youthful flirtatiousness. Could it have been this jealousy that drove Mary to imprison Elizabeth in the Tower for 3 months, on the pretext of Elizabeth's involvement in a plot following protests against Mary's plans to marry Philip? Apparently, Philip interceded with Mary on Elizabeth's behalf - did he actually have a hidden agenda as a result of his dalliances with Elizabeth?

The themes of jealousy and loneliness which Kate had felt also featured frequently in my other sessions with her. Indeed, Kate later wrote to me that the sadness and loneliness from Mary's life still lingered with her many months after she'd first felt them in our regressions.

Chapter 15

My Scepticism Finally Dissolves

It was in our next session together that any lingering doubts which I still possessed about Kate actually being the reincarnation of Mary vanished, as a result of the very specific details which she came up with whilst in trance. She began by picking up once more on her fraught relationship with Elizabeth.

> *"I'm having an argument with Elizabeth. I'm shorter than she is. She's really cross and banging her arms down because I told her off. I'm saying 'you're nothing but a whore'. She's shouting 'you don't know what you're talking about because you're a dried-up old maid.' I feel really angry."*

Her face was stern throughout this then she softened for a few moments as she moved onto another memory. She became tense again:

> *"Someone's brought a plate with a letter on it. I read it as I walk down a gallery - it's on the second floor and has leaded glass panes. To the left are paintings, tapestries and wooden panels. There's a fireplace in the middle of the room. The name Framlingham comes to mind. It's cold and marshy but I think it's where I live. I feel that one of my servants is a black boy. I'm waiting for some news. A man comes in and says 'are you alright my lady?' I feel anxious but I tell him that I'm fine. I'm anxious about some news. It's got to be sorted out as I don't want any bloodshed."*

I asked Kate to become aware of the cause of the anxiety.

"It's about Lady Jane Grey. I've got my supporters camped outside the castle - Framlingham. She's dead, they've executed her. I'm Queen - there's no bloodshed. I was waiting to hear if there was going to be any trouble amongst the people. I thought there might be an uprising."

As I heard Kate recounting this it didn't really mean very much to me as at that time I'd not studied or read much about the Tudor period or the life of Queen Mary. It was only later, as I began preparing my notes for this book, that I read a couple of biographies on Mary. I was astonished to find that Kate was reporting Mary's reactions to real historical events. In 1553, shortly after her brother Edward's death whilst King, there was a plot to oust Mary before her coronation and to crown Lady Jane Grey as Queen. The conspiracy was led by John Dudley, Earl of Warwick who gathered an army together in London. Mary rallied her forces at Framlingham Castle in Suffolk, where many thousands of men joined her and surrounded the castle walls in readiness to defend her. How Kate could have known this without some prior knowledge of the period I do not know, unless she was actually re-experiencing them in a past life as Mary.

The next memory she moved to again brought in a specific piece of information in the shape of a name of someone who I'd never heard of and I'm quite sure few others have either unless they've studied Tudor history. Again, she became anxious as she shared with me her feelings:

"I feel as if I'm being crowned. I have a heavy crown on my head and it feels uncomfortable. There are lots of people around and I'm in a cathedral. It's my coronation. I feel like I want to cry, it's a heavy burden being Queen and I'm scared. I want to be good and fair and make changes but I'm petrified and happy at the same time. I've waited for this and I wanted it but I'm no longer free. I know that

there are many enemies waiting for me to make one wrong move. Cardinal Pole is on my side - I think I can trust him. They all want me to get married so there's an heir but I'm quite old now. I feel as if I'm in my thirties. Elizabeth is on the sidelines waiting for me to trip up, and she has her supporters. How I used to love that girl but I hate her now. She's manipulative and she wants rid of me. I want to rule like my father."

Having checked with the history books, I find that the reference Kate made to Cardinal Pole was a very significant one. Cardinal Pole was Henry VIII's Archbishop of Canterbury until he was banished in exile abroad during the Reformation. Like Mary he was a practising Catholic who supported the reintroduction of Catholicism into Britain once Mary was on the throne. He was in constant contact with Mary for some years after she became Queen and his advice was always highly regarded by her (it was said at the time that Mary had more regard for Pole than for all the members of her council put together). His support and influence were deeply meaningful to her and he returned to England during Mary's reign to act as one of her advisers.

I was amazed when I found out that this supported Kate's words about him-*"he's on my side - I think I can trust him."* How could an ordinary housewife from suburban England who knew so little about English history have even known the name of Cardinal Pole let alone his close connection with Mary?

Kate then moved onto another memory, again exhibiting signs of dread and discomfort as she lay in trance, once more containing details only known to students of history:

"They're trying to marry me off. I'm sick of it. I can't trust anyone and I feel so lonely. Philip despises me. I'm older than he is and he's so handsome. I'm no good in the bedchamber. He flirts with the other ladies, especially Elizabeth. I love him but I can't make him happy. I was so happy when we got married, but the happiness didn't last

long. I thought I'd got a mate, someone to get rid of the loneliness, but that's still there. I feel so sad. He just helps me with political things, and everyone at court is waiting for me to have a child."

After all the tension she'd experienced, Kate finished the session on a gentler note, a memory that brought her a sense of relief:

"I'm out riding in the crisp, autumnal air. It's an escape - I like riding".

Very much like her sister Elizabeth, Mary used horse riding as a means to let off steam and to relax. The session ended with me still in two minds as to whether or not I could believe that Kate really was Mary Tudor, but my subsequent research into her memories has me convinced that she was indeed Queen Mary I.

Chapter 16

More Specific Facts

In our next session Kate brought up a variety of memories from Mary's life, on the face of it none of them of great significance but each of which validated for me that Kate really was the reincarnation of Mary as the information she gave was confirmed by my subsequent research into Mary's life. None of the things that she came up with could be known without some knowledge of the Queen's life, and remember Kate had not studied the period in any way.

Once she was in trance and I'd guided her back into the past life, she sighed and began speaking quietly:

"I'm opening a big wooden door with round handles to lift the catch up. The top of the door is round. I step down a stone step into a room with small square tiles - it's probably a turret room. There's a fireplace opposite the door and leaded glass windows. It's like a small private chamber with tapestries on the walls. I'm alone and I sit at a writing table. I feel hungry but I'm telling myself I mustn't eat anything. It feels weird, I feel short and petite and I feel I have really long ankles and I'm wearing little pointed shoes. I don't want to eat because I don't want to get fat. Elizabeth's got a beautiful figure and I don't want to get fat and frumpy, so I want to stay as thin as I can be with a narrow waist. I'm in my 20's. I wanted to be slim before Elizabeth became an issue.

I'm in another room now and my ladies are getting me ready. I can feel my narrow waist. They're curling my long hair, which is gingery-brown. I feel like I'm standing tall with an air of dignity, and I'm enjoying feeling hungry.

Now I've gone into a banqueting hall and I have my hand on top of a gentleman's hand as we are entering. I sit at the head of the table and there's lots of chatter with people enjoying themselves. I don't want to eat the food and so I'm just picking and eating morsels.

I've moved to another scene now. I'm in a courtyard garden with roses all around. I want to go for a horse-ride later. I like to do that so I can feel free. My father liked hunting - I remember him talking about it. I hunted with him when I was very young, when he was still with my mother." At this point Kate began to cry. *"I miss my mother. I feel we were banished away from him and we had a poor life compared to when we were with him. The new living conditions were not regal enough for my mother. I feel I had a very strong bond with her. She was very kind. She didn't say such horrible things about the Boleyn girl as the other people did."* After a pause she went on. *"I've got a headache. I'm poorly now and mother's mopping my brow. She's asked father to come and see me (we're in banishment) but he won't. I've been asking for him to come but he won't. I don't know what I've done to be so bad that he won't come. Mother says it's not me but I feel like it's my fault. She's so kind. I feel as if the court wants me to go away from her as well. I feel muddled. I mustn't eat. I'll starve to death and that'll serve father right. If he won't come and see me I won't be here anymore. I hate him for not coming. I can remember when I was really small sitting on his knee and pulling his beard. He had kind eyes. My mother loved him so much, but I feel we're poor now and cold".*

Even though totally factual (once more Kate was completely correct in what she reported) I found these memories of Henry and the exile of his wife and daughter callous in the extreme, so I asked Kate if she could remember what happened when her father died.

"I feel pleased. He tried to reconcile with all of us - me, Elizabeth and Edward, and to bring us all together again. After the way he treated me he thinks he can put it all right, yet he'd had me called a

bastard when the other children came along. I tolerate him but I can never forgive him. I want to say Elizabeth's a slimy, little creep, fluttering her eyelids around father and pretending everything's alright. Edward's a quiet, sullen boy. Father looks old and he has a bad leg. I'm knelt at the side of his chair and he has his feet up on a stool. I have to feel sorry for him".

The facts that Kate gave me can be verified by the history books. Mary was said to be 'thin' and 'spare' by contemporary commentators, and her early banishment together with her mother Katherine of Aragon by the King had a great impact on her. In her early childhood Henry VIII was very close to her and when he sent her and Katherine into exile she was probably so damaged emotionally that the scars of his betrayal remained with her for the rest of her life. To go from being a royal princess to being labelled 'the King's bastard' at Henry's insistence must have been excruciating for the young Mary. No wonder, as Kate stated, that she could never forgive him, even when he allowed her to return to court in her early teens.

Kate's next visit to my office once more brought more surprises in the form of further memories that only a student of Mary Tudor's life would have known about, reinforcing the belief I now hold that Kate had indeed been Queen Mary. Once in trance she began by feeling pain in her stomach:

"It feels as if I'm pregnant. I'm wearing a dark, charcoal grey, velvet dress and I'm holding my stomach with my hands. I'm alone, indoors, looking out of a window which is triangular leaded into gardens below with clipped, yew hedges. I feel content because of the baby but lonely because Philip's away, he's not in England. I always feel lonely when he's not there. I talk to my ladies-in-waiting but there are spies and I don't know who you can really trust. I feel quite sick. Later on when I'm pregnant I'm all shut up and alone, as if I'm in confinement. I feel I should keep the curtains shut but I don't like

to be shut in and I want to look at the garden. They tell me that it's best to be on my own to rest. I feel pain in my stomach and there's blood and the physician and some of my ladies are there. I'm not pregnant anymore. I've lost the baby. I feel like I've let everybody down and I'm too embarrassed to show myself."

At this point Kate became emotional, wringing her hands together whilst her face contorted with pain and sadness:

"Philip's not there. I feel all alone. I just want to shut myself away. I don't want to face anybody anymore, I feel I'll be the laughing stock of the people. I feel so unhappy and depressed, but I'm expected to carry on as if nothing has happened. I know now that if there's a next time that will be an end of me. Elizabeth will gloat on it. I feel that she's sitting on the sidelines, watching and waiting for me to fail at everything. She's so beautiful and can get what she wants and whom she wants. She lifts up her skirt and they all trot after her, including Philip. I feel angry and jealous. I loved her so much as a child but father's death changed things. She and Edward were close and I was pushed out. Before then, either I was the bastard or she was the bastard. They said Father wasn't married legally so they called me a bastard. Mother was frightened of having her head chopped off, and they called her a bastard too. Father had sex with both the Boleyn women".

According to historical accounts, a few months after marrying Philip, Mary did believe she was pregnant and entered, as was customary in those days, a period of confinement. After several months of apparent pregnancy it was finally announced that she was not pregnant. What had happened is unknown, with some historians believing that she simply had had a phantom pregnancy, but one contemporary source certainly has it that 'the Queen was delivered of a mole or lump of flesh, and was in great peril of death'. Could it be that this is what Kate had experienced? Kate was also accurate in knowing that Philip spent a great deal of their marriage apart from Mary, causing Mary a lot of unhappiness. She was, as a result of the traumas in her childhood, what we would nowadays call 'needy' in her relationship.

I was surprised too when I looked into Kate's claims that Katherine, Mary's mother, like her was also called a bastard during the time when Henry VIII was trying to divorce her. I was even more amazed when I looked into Kate's words 'father had sex with both Boleyn girls' and found that to be absolutely true. Anne Boleyn, for whom Henry divorced Katherine of Aragon, had an elder sister who was Henry's mistress at court for a number of years until Anne became the object of his affections. How could Kate have known all of this?

The remainder of the session also brought up details which I later checked in history books and found to be correct. Kate relaxed after the pains of the miscarriage, and her face became sad:

> *"I'm on a boat, going to the Tower and I feel really upset, as if I want to cry. I'm going there to see somebody and I feel I've got the power to let someone out. It's a man and I want to say that he should never have been there in the first place. He's an elderly man and I give him a big hug. The name Gardiner comes to me and I feel he has a high position and he's been imprisoned there because of his beliefs."*

Imagine my utter astonishment when I found that Gardiner really was a highly significant figure in Mary's life. Stephen Gardiner was Bishop of Winchester until Henry VIII incarcerated him in the Tower for his Catholic beliefs, which were contrary to the King's adoption of Protestantism. Soon after the abortive uprising by Dudley had collapsed Mary rode to London from Framlingham in great procession to lay claim to her right as Queen of England. As she arrived in London she made her way to the Tower where she greeted Gardiner and two other men who had been falsely imprisoned by her father. As they knelt to ask her pardon it's reported that 'she came to them and kissed them and said "these be my prisoners"'. How on earth could Kate have known this? I was gob-smacked when I found that this little known episode in Mary's life was true.

We finished the session with Kate experiencing a lot of sadness as she remembered the reason why Mary became known as 'Bloody Mary'. She became emotional and sobbed bitterly as she told me:

"I didn't mean to put those people to death. I didn't want to harm them. My religious leaders told me it was the best way to stop the rebellion and those people had to conform for us to have a Catholic State, but I don't like it. I'm proud of my religion but I can't let them see that I'm weak. I mustn't be weak. I'm back in my rooms, alone. I don't mean to be a cruel person but I just want to be strong like my father".

Kate came out of trance, still feeling sad and much aware of the great loneliness she had experienced as Mary endeavoured to be as strong a monarch as her father.

Chapter 17

The Pain Finally Released

My final session with Kate took place a little while after the previous ones, so we both had chance to process the information which she'd remembered, but although in the meantime I'd done some research which verified for me that Kate was indeed the reincarnation of Mary, Kate herself had rigorously stayed away from all possible sources of Mary's life. However, although I was by now more 'clued - up' about Tudor and Elizabethan history, as usual I didn't bring any of my knowledge into the session in order that my questions to Kate whilst she was in trance would not be seen to be leading her in any way. I was scrupulous in asking simple, open, 'clean' questions. Once she was relaxing in hypnosis, I asked her sub-conscious to take her back to the past life that we'd been exploring, and after a few moments during which she regressed back through the centuries, Kate began to share memories which I would guess were from quite late in Mary's life:

"I'm back in the rose garden and I've picked a pink rose and I can smell its' pleasant, heady smell. It's early morning and I'm alone. I'm always alone and it makes me feel so sad. I feel safe in the garden, nobody can spoil things here. There are buildings all around with the rose garden in the centre, but members of the court can still see me in here. They're always waiting for me to trip up, I just can't trust anybody. They know what you're thinking if you let them in, but I'm the Queen and the loneliness has always been there, even as a child. I remember I was always fearful, but when I was really young it was beautiful and we had pretty things. Then I was taken away and it went cold and dark. There was that whore-bitch who I think wanted

us dead to keep us out of the way. She strutted around and I hated her. They were cruel to my mother when she was Queen. She was so beautiful - they threw her away - they threw us both away. Where we were sent to live was more bare - I can see bricks on the walls with no tapestries on them."

Kate's tone throughout was melancholic and she frequently sighed as she recounted the misery of childhood, feeling the bitter cruelty of Henry in not seeing his daughter for long periods of time, only finally bringing her back into court long after her mother had died.

"There was only one nice thing and that was the house where we lived had grass which went down to the water and I could go out on the grass to play. I felt free down there. Either we had a dog or the people we lived with had a dog. We lived in a house belonging to other people and it was not lavish. They spied on us as well, they never stopped spying on us. I wished the whore-bitch was dead so that father could come back to us. Then she had her whore sister. They were so pretty. Philip trots after her, she swishes her skirt and he runs after her, like a dog on heat."

Kate paused for a while and was quiet, her face sad and her sighs symptoms of the unhappiness she was feeling. From what she had told me so far, it appeared that she was looking back on the life from a time near the end of it. Eventually she continued:

"I'm sitting indoors on a chair with a velvet-like blanket, gazing through the window. In the corner is a lady-in-waiting doing some tapestry. The sunlight's streaming in as I look across the courtyard and the flowers. I feel you can get to this place by water as well. I feel really tired. I feel like I always feel, lost and alone. No matter what I do, it's never right. It's so hard. They said it would help to change things, but I've got all their deaths on my hands." She

began to cry. *"They burned them. They said if we showed them what would happen they would conform, but it doesn't matter how many, they won't conform. I had to show I was strong but inside it's eating me up. I didn't want to kill them, but I wanted to show them I was strong".*

By this stage Kate was sobbing violently, her hands wringing together as if tormented and the sound of her voice betrayed the intensity of the agony and remorse she was feeling.

"They said they'd conform if I showed them I was strong. I couldn't let them see it was hurting me, I couldn't let them see I was weak. Oh God forgive me, what have I done? All I wanted to do was to bring the faith back. That and to be loved. Oh God forgive me. There was no love, my life was empty. Why have I got this burden?"

Kate almost screamed out these last words as she experienced an emotional catharsis much stronger than anything I'd seen in my previous regressions with her. I sat quietly, softly reassuring her that it was OK for her to feel and release the emotions, allowing her to let go of the emotional pain that she'd had stored inside her all of her life without realising it was there and the effect it had had upon her in this life. It took a while, but eventually her sobbing eased and she relaxed again. I asked her to move to the time of the death in that life, and whereas before she had been animated her speech now came slowly, some of the words slurred:

"I feel a heavy weariness, much worse than it used to be. I'm laid on a couch. Such heaviness and I feel bloated. I've embarrassed myself again like I did before. I thought I was having a baby but there wasn't one and I was so embarrassed. I so wanted a baby. He'd have come back to me if there was a baby. I haven't seen him for months and I love him so much. I've let everyone down because I've got no-

one to follow me. I feel I've failed. I've failed at everything." Kate began to cry again, feeling the bleakness of her legacy as she lay on her death-bed. *"I feel so empty and I'm ashamed I've left no heir. I've lost Philip and I've lost Calais in France. It was our last stronghold and we lost the battle as we tried to keep it. I've failed. He won't come back, I've written to him. I feel so sick and bloated. I'm just wearing a night-shift, being sick into a large black bowl. Why do I deserve this? I feel so tired and ill. I'm praying to God and asking him if Elizabeth will take on the faith. If she doesn't it'll all have been for nothing. I've been writing to my friend, Cardinal Pole. I feel I had to try and bring myself to show affection to Elizabeth, but it's very hard to do. Towards the end I had to give her some of my jewellery to show the people I loved her as she is the Queen-in-waiting, but I hated her and I had to pretend to like her".*

I asked Kate what had been the reason for the hatred.

"When she was 15 or 16 she was so beautiful and I felt so ugly next to her and then the way father treated her, giving her affection and love. I felt the outsider."

Kate sighed deeply, and was silent for some time. Her voice had been getting softer as she approached the end of the life as Mary and her words had been gradually becoming more and more slurred. After several minutes of quiet, she breathed a long, deep breath and finally spoke:

"I'm peaceful now, it's over. My friend joins me not long after I died. He was my true friend, a special man whom I could trust. I feel really sad, I loved Philip so much but he didn't love me, and I think he had her lined up for after I died. All I wanted was his love. He wasn't with me when I died."

With those words we ended the session. Kate was pensive afterwards, still feeling the bleakness of Mary's last hours. The overwhelming feelings which she took away from the experiences she had felt as Mary was loneliness and despair. Mary, who desperately had wanted to be loved by someone, had died as she had lived, unloved and alone.

Again, after the regression I checked with histories of Mary which recounted in depth her last days, and once more was amazed to find that Kate had remembered details which are only available to students of the period. These are as follows: firstly, Philip was not present during her final illness, staying in Spain and corresponding with her by letter. As Kate said, he was trying to manipulate Elizabeth to change her faith so she could marry him and rule Britain as his Queen after Mary's death. Secondly, in January 1558 (a few months prior to Mary's death in November) Calais, the last English stronghold on French soil, was captured by French troops who claimed it back into French territory. Apparently there was a tradition that its loss was the major regret of Mary's life. Thirdly, as Mary began to make plans for her passing during her illness, she sent to Elizabeth her 'rich and precious' jewels and to ask her to promise to uphold the Catholic faith. Fourthly, a few hours after Mary's death, her friend and trusted advisor, Cardinal Pole also died after a long illness.

As well as this, Mary was of course known as 'Bloody Mary' due to the vicious way that Protestants were put down during her reign, often with mass burnings of people who refused to practise as Catholics. Could it really be that Mary was reluctant to order the executions, being pressured to do so by her advisers? Kate's extreme emotion whilst reliving this seemed to suggest she was.

For myself, a moderately intelligent bloke with a general knowledge of English history, I was not aware of these facts until I read some biographies of Mary. As I've previously stated, Kate had done no reading or research into Mary's life so there could be no way that she could have been aware of such specific information regarding Mary's last days. For me, the only way that she would have known these details was if she was actually re-experiencing them in the form of distant memories held in her subconscious mind. I do believe that Kate is indeed the reincarnation of Mary Tudor.

POSTSCRIPT

After we'd finished our exploration of Mary's life, I asked Kate to write her impressions of the regressions, and how it felt to know that she is the reincarnation of such a famous person. Her thoughts are as follows:

When I first heard my 'name' called deep down I 'knew' I was Princess Mary, playing with my siblings Elizabeth and Edward. The bond felt very strong but I thought I was being presumptuous, so I tried to play down what I felt as I didn't want to appear egotistical, in other words I must be the lady-in-waiting or the maidservant. However, throughout several more sessions Mary came out stronger and stronger until I could hide her no more.

Oh a Queen! Wow, what a past life. How great one would think when comparing that life with today's. Monarchy, money, jewels, beautiful clothes etc, but I have never felt so sad, unloved, lonely, desperate, ashamed, filled with fear, an all-consuming fear of life or death. A life with no privacy at all, no trust, not allowing oneself to be seen as your true self; in fear that all those around are waiting to seize their moment, having to hide 'Mary', a girl, a woman just wanting love and companionship from her father and her husband. The only solace seemed to be walking round the rose garden and riding.

It has made me feel so lucky in this life time. Yes I am no one 'special', but I can be 'me' and following the regressions, I have forged my personal identity more and more, allowing my true self to shine through. Some big traits though, have come through from the past life, including liking 'nice' things and architecture, also I have a very expensive 'eye', and I am sure I can be a secret snob!!

Before the regressions if you had asked me 'who do you think you were in the Tudor times'? I would have said Queen Elizabeth I, because as a child I would trot round the playground aged about 8 years old saying I was Queen Elizabeth, as my middle name is Elizabeth and I was born and she died on the 24th March! I had never read anything about Mary or Henry VIII prior to my regressions and I still haven't just in case I am regressed again. The only information about Elizabeth I and Henry VIII, was what I learnt at junior school and going to the pictures in the 1970's to see films about them.

After the sessions I felt very subdued when travelling home, I kept thinking 'could it be true what was coming out about Mary'? I had accepted other life times I had experienced during regression, so why not this one? Mixed emotions came up, including the feeling of not being worthy of being 'royal' in this present life; embarrassment of being famous; and excitement of being a Queen. Eventually I seemed to make sense of the information over time, but I think if I'd been making it all up I would have chosen a more glamorous past life person!

Chapter 18

A Victorian Murder Victim

The next two 'characters' I present to you are shorter in scope than those featured so far, but I think are no less fascinating in the stories they tell.

Jane came to me for therapy to help her with a heap of emotional baggage she was finding difficult to carry and which was preventing her from living her life freely or effectively. A policewoman, she had endured a lot of difficult and broken relationships and her self-confidence and self-esteem were very low. As she spoke to me of her past she appeared nervous and unhappy with life. Once we'd finished discussing her background she agreed that she was ready to undergo hypnosis to see if we could uncover the real roots of her emotional instabilities. Once she was in trance I asked her subconscious to create a signalling response that it could use to unconsciously signal 'yes' or 'no' to my questions (the Ideo-Motor Response previously mentioned). When I asked the questions her entire left hand rose in the air all by itself and indicated that the roots of her problems lay in 5 previous lifetimes.

Although I only saw Jane for a few sessions it was the first past life that she experienced that was a real shocker and one which falls within the remit of this book on famous past lives. With her eyes closed in trance, Jane began to shiver as she recounted a miserable existence in Victorian London:

"I'm a little girl, about 6 years of age. I feel unloved. I'm in a workhouse or a factory and I'm so tired, being made to work so hard. I'm not wearing any shoes and my feet are sore and dirty. I'm really hungry all the time. I don't go outside much."

After a pause, she continued:

> *"I've moved on in time now. I'm about 14 years old. I'm in a market place, in a street. I've run away and I'm trying to hide. I don't want to go back to the workhouse. I want to be like the ladies going past. Other girls tell me I can make money. I stay with one of them and she gives me some clothes. I start doing favours for blokes, for wealthy gents, doctors and the like. It makes you feel dirty and it's dangerous sometimes when you get a good smack. I don't make much money."* Jane sighed and her voice quivered. *"I just want to be loved and be taken care of. I turn to drink. My health's not good. People tell me to sort myself out."*

I have to say that although all this was interesting there was nothing unusual in Jane's story, as I have regressed other people into past lives where they have relived lives as prostitutes, usually remembering sordid and squalid existences. I asked her to move on to the next significant time in that life. She moved on several years and it was what she said next that made me sit up and listen intently.

> *"I've moved on and I'm quite a lot older now. I'm outdoors and it's night time. I'm in a street and it's dark and wet. I'm standing alone and I feel frightened, like someone's watching me. The girls have told me to watch out - the Ripper's about. Some girls have been murdered. We should go round in two's or three's."* Jane started to shiver. *"There's a man in a dark cloak. He's bearded and possibly in his 30's. He's smartly dressed and he's got a watch and chain on. He's wearing gloves. He takes his watch out and looks at the time. He asks me if I'm open for business, he says he hasn't much time as he has to be somewhere."* I asked Jane about the sound of his voice. *"He's well-to-do. I have a bad feeling about him. We walk and he grabs me from behind and drags me into a dark alley nearby. He's pulled me to the floor backwards. I'm screaming but nobody's*

coming. He's really strong. He's got a knife or something. I feel pain across my throat - he's cut my throat. I feel my strength going away from me and I feel like I can't breathe. There's pain and I can feel a wet coldness on my cheek. There's a smell of drains. I can't move. I keep thinking 'why me? I've not done anything to anybody.' I don't know him - he doesn't like women. I'm thinking that they told me so, I shouldn't have been there, I should have listened. Everyone was talking about the man, it wasn't his first time. But I needed the money." Jane sighed and was silent for a couple of minutes. Then she spoke softly: *"I'm outside my body. It's peaceful now."*

As a therapist I usually find that the shock and brutality of such a death has the potential to cause both physical and emotional problems in this life so we spent some time releasing the negative feelings Jane was holding in her body from the trauma of the death at the hands of Jack the Ripper, in order to free her from the negative effects it had had upon her in her present lifetime. It may also be that Jane's string of broken relationships (some of them violent) were symbolic of her unconscious ability to draw towards her the wrong type of person, someone who would harm her in some way, much as she'd unconsciously drawn Jack the Ripper to her in her previous life.

Although I was fascinated by Jane's account, I was still sceptical as she had not given me any information which was particularly specific and so it was possible that she had imagined the experience. My last question to her before we finished the session was to ask her if she could remember her name in the past life. Without a moment's hesitation she gave me a name which at that time meant nothing to me but which upon subsequent investigation proved to be spot on: *"Catherine Eddowes."*

I brought Jane out of trance and after we had talked for a while about what she had experienced we finished the session and Jane left my office. I went on to one of the many Jack the Ripper web-sites on the Internet and was shocked to find that

Catherine Eddowes was indeed one of his victims. The 'Whitechapel Murders' as they became known took place in the East End of London between August 1888 and February 1891 in which women allegedly working as prostitutes were violently murdered and their bodies horribly mutilated. Although there is uncertainty as to whether all the murders were committed by one person, it is universally agreed that 5 of them were the work of a single killer. Catherine Eddowes was one of those five.

She was born in Wolverhampton on April 14th 1842 and at the time of her death was 5 feet tall with hazel-green eyes and dark auburn hair. She had a tattoo in blue ink on her left forearm "TC" (probably the initials of one of her common-law husbands, Thomas Conway) and was suffering form Bright's disease. Friends spoke of Catherine as an intelligent, scholarly woman but one who was possessed of a fierce temper. Her adult life appears to have been one of gradual decline. She had 3 children to Thomas Conway but she took to drink and split from the family in 1880. A year later she was living with a new partner called John Kelly at Cooney's common lodging-house at 55 Flower and Dean Street, Spitalfields, which was known as being at the heart of London's most notorious criminal areas. Here she took to casual prostitution to pay the rent. She was killed on Sunday 30th September 1888 and her body was found in Mitre Square in the City of London. Her throat had been severed by two cuts and her abdomen was ripped open by a long, deep jagged wound, and her left kidney and much of her uterus had been removed. A mortuary photograph of her clearly shows the severity of the attack, including the depth of the wound to the throat.

Her last hours and death have been well documented. At 8.30pm on Saturday 29th September she was found lying in the road drunk on Aldgate High Street by PC Louis Robinson and taken into custody at Bishopgate police station. She was released at 1am on the morning of Sunday 30th and she was last seen alive half an hour later by 3 witnesses who saw her talking with a man (probably her killer) at the entrance to Church Passage (which leads to Mitre Square). Only 10 minutes later her mutilated body was found by a policeman on his beat.

I realise that from Jane's information we are unable to glean the identity of the Ripper, but I think it is interesting that the details she gave just before she experienced the murder does fit in with suspicions that experts have as to the identity of the Ripper. Jane stated that he was a well-to-do man, and the removal of internal organs from 3 of the murder victims has led some to propose that the killer possessed anatomical or surgical knowledge, which would indeed mean that he was likely to be from the upper classes of society at that time. This possibility was first mooted by police surgeon Dr. Frederick Gordon Brown who stated in his post-mortem report on Catherine Eddowes: "I believe that the perpetrator of the act must have had considerable knowledge of the position of the organs in the abdominal cavity and the way of removing them. It required a great deal of knowledge to have removed the kidney and to know where it was placed." Jane also felt that she was dragged into an alley, which also fits in with what is known of the murder.

Maybe Jane's career as a policewoman in this life was no accident, but a direct response to her horrific death in that lifetime. After all of the thousands of books and articles written about the Ripper murders over the last 130 years, I think that this is the closest anyone has been to seeing the face of Jack the Ripper. A chilling thought if ever there was one.

Chapter 19

A Brave Airman

Tom's case is an interesting one, although strictly speaking it falls outside the 'Famous Past Lives' frame of reference witnessed so far. This is because Tom's past life personality was not in himself famous, but took part in one of the most famous events that occurred during World War Two.

Tom and his wife Mary came to me after they had taken part in a past life meditation session as part of a spiritual development group they were attending. In the meditation session Tom had visions of being a crew member in a Lancaster bomber, which he felt had taken part in the Dambusters raid. Both Tom and Mary had very strong feelings afterwards that they had been in the past life together in some way, and they wanted to find out whether what he had seen was a real past life and if so had they indeed known each other in it.

We discussed how much Tom had envisioned in his meditation session and he told me that he had not experienced it in any deep way, but he felt he had been killed in a bombing raid at some point. He was keen to make sense out of what he had seen. I took Tom into trance and once he was relaxing I guided him back into the past in his thoughts, and asked his subconscious to take him back into the last lifetime before this present incarnation. He saw himself as a man, standing alone outside, wearing black polished boots, an air force blue uniform and an officer's cap. I allowed him to settle into the character by remaining quiet for a few moments, before I asked him what was happening.

"It's dark, and I'm sitting inside an aircraft on the ground, waiting for take-off. I'm a wireless operator." After a pause, he continued: *"We've taken off. It's a clear night. We're heading out towards Germany. There's nothing for me to do. We've got complete radio silence."*

Tom looked tense as he lay in the chair, and was silent for some time, as if reliving the tension of being on the mission as the plane flew over enemy territory. He then spoke excitedly:

"Some guns on the ground open up. We're hit on the port wing. We're losing altitude. We're not high anyway, we're only just skimming the tree tops. We're coming down. We hit something on the way down. We're a long way from the target. We've not attacked anything - we still have the bomb. The pilot's trying to keep it in the air. We're panicking as we're going down, out of control. We hit the ground. Pain in my head and legs. Then peace. There was nothing he could do to stop it happening. He's a friend from Australia - Captain Norman Barlow. Although the plane's destroyed the bomb doesn't go off. "

Tom sighed deeply and was quiet for some time. I assumed he had died and was in the spirit and so I asked Tom, if he could become aware of his name in that lifetime. After a few moments he replied:

"Williams. Flying Officer Williams. I think I'm married to Gwen or Gwendolyn. I don't think we have any children."

I then asked him to move to another significant time in that life, before the final raid in which he perished.

"I'm in Australia, before the war. I'm in my work clothes, working with sheep. It's before I signed up. There are sheep all around. I

enjoy the work but there's no money in it. There's no satisfaction in working for nothing. There's no future in this. I have to decide on an alternative way of life. I'm discussing with another man - I think he's my father - what I'm going to do. I get no bad feelings from him but it distresses me to leave the farm. I'm drawn to join the armed forces, but there's somebody else I have to consider - Gwen." Tom sighed again. *"I hadn't really thought about her, I'm just doing it for myself. We're both upset when I tell her. I think she's my wife. I feel all churned up, I don't want to go but I have a sense of resignation, knowing I have to go. I feel a lot of emotions. I feel sadness and fear when I think of the danger I might be involved in. My mother's devastated when she finds out I'm leaving and going to Europe, she doesn't want me to go."*

I asked Tom to move onto any other wartime experiences he may have had. He felt himself flying on an aircraft again.

"We're on a different type of mission, flying much higher. We have the protection of other bombers around us, so it feels safer. I'm the wireless operator. We're attacking a city in Germany. There are no dramas, we just take it as routine. We get to the target area, drop bombs and turn back for home."

After another period of silence, Tom spoke again:

"We're on another raid, and someone's been injured. I'm not sure if it's the flight engineer or a gunner but they've been badly injured, maybe killed or badly wounded. Possibly they've been hit by a German fighter. So I leave my position and take over. I think I go up into the cockpit and help the pilot control the plane - it feels like it's Barlow again. I'm not sure if this happens when we're in a previous squadron, before we join 617 Squadron."

We were approaching the end of the session and as Tom

appeared to be finding it harder to get information from the past life we closed things down and I brought him back to full awareness. He was surprised at experiencing so much and although he had never read anything specifically about the Dambusters raid he told me that he had always been fascinated by military aircraft and he had always had a desire to visit Australia. As well as this he had had an interest in agriculture for as long as he could remember. He could still feel some of the emotion relating to Gwen, who he had a strong feeling is his wife Mary in this present lifetime. He felt he had done something to hurt or upset her in some way, and he had a deep sense of regret for what he thought was through some form of selfishness.

Some time after our past life session, Tom came to see me to show me a book he had since bought on the Dambusters raid, as he wanted to see if any of the information he had remembered was real. Entitled 'Australia's Dambusters' by historian and author Colin Burgess (no relation), the book gives a great deal of detail about the raid from the perspective of the 13 Australian airmen who took part in the mission. We found that a great deal of Tom's experience whilst in trance was backed up by historical fact. Firstly, Tom had said that they had taken off on a clear night. This was indeed the case. On the night of 16th May 1943 nineteen Lancaster bombers of 617 Squadron (which had been modified to carry Barnes Wallis' recently invented 'bouncing bombs') took off from Scampton airfield in Lincolnshire in 3 waves with the intention of flying at a low level over Holland to destroy three dams in the Ruhr valley in Northern Germany. There were 13 Australians in the three formations. One of them was listed as Flying Officer C.R. Williams. Charlie Williams was born in Queensland in 1909 and like his father was a sheep farmer. A combination of the Depression and the start of the war saw him sign up with the RAAF at the age of 31, training to be a wireless operator/gunner. Flight Lieutenant Norman Barlow was his pilot on this most famous of wartime combat missions, with Williams acting as wireless operator.

So far, so good. Everything Tom had remembered whilst in trance had a solid basis in reality. That would be incredible enough, but he also came up with specific information about the raid itself which also featured in the book. The first Lancaster to take off was Norman Barlow's, flying across the North Sea with the objective of bombing the Sorpe dam. Unfortunately, as they flew low over Germany it is believed they hit a pylon and crashed into a field, with no survivors. This is very much in keeping with Tom's account, although he felt they had been hit by flak before 'we hit something on the way down' (possibly a pylon?). Possibly the most amazing thing that Tom had mentioned was that the bomb they were carrying did not explode when they crashed, and this was exactly what happened. Colin Burgess' book actually has a photograph of the bomb after its recovery by Nazi soldiers!

So much of Tom's experience fitted almost completely with the facts, including some highly specific details, that I find it highly unlikely that Tom could have known without studying books or articles about the raid, which he assured me he had never done. Surely the only reasonable explanation is that he truly did live in his previous life as Flying Officer Charles Williams, dying in the early hours of the 17th May 1943 as part of 617 Squadron's highly successful mission to damage the German war machine.

Chapter 20

'I'm just going outside'......

As with all of the cases presented here in this book, my next famous past life character came completely out of the blue and was not expected in any way, either by my client Alan or myself. Alan came to me as a result of childhood trauma which he felt had resulted in giving him low self-confidence throughout his life. A 40-something self-employed business man, on the surface self-reliant and running a successful retail outlet, he was intelligent, articulate and witty, although throughout our initial interview he avoided eye contact and seemed genuinely shy. He seemed sad as he spoke of certain events in his childhood which had affected him, but there was no outward show of emotion as he did so. Having discussed his past history we moved into the hypnosis section of our first session, and he went nicely into trance and began to relax deeply. As is my usual practice, I elicited an Ideo Motor Response so that his subconscious could answer yes or no to my questions by moving one of his fingers, and I began to ask his subconscious about the root causes of his lack of confidence. It responded by indicating that his childhood did indeed contain Significant Emotional Events that were connected to causing his issues, but it also signalled that there were two past lives which contained traumatic events that he'd brought into this present life which were affecting him. His subconscious then indicated that it would be OK for us to explore the 'causal events' in order to help him to feel stronger. As we'd run out of time we ended the session at that point, with the agreement that we'd start exploring the past traumas in hypnosis in our next session. Alan came out of trance and looked amazed at what had happened. Not only had his finger been moving all by itself, but it had indicated two past lives needed to be worked through. He expressed scepticism about the concept of past lives. He had very little knowledge of the concept of reincarnation, and no belief in such a thing. However, he agreed that he would remain open–minded if that would help him to feel better in himself as a result of the therapy.

My experience is that lack of confidence is usually a fear-based issue. When we have low self-esteem and low self-confidence it usually means that the person doesn't feel safe in the world, feeling insecure inside themselves and frightened in the world. This fear comes as a result of events (both in this life and previous lives) which have bothered, disturbed or traumatised them, leaving an energy of fear in the subconscious mind. The person then responds to this fear energy by feeling unsafe as they live their lives. Releasing the fear by reliving the causal traumas is one way in which regression therapy works.

Alan returned the following week and we began a process, over several sessions, of reliving the events from this present life which had so upset him in childhood. During that time he began to feel measurably better. His subconscious seemed to want to work only on this lifetime, so we allowed that process to take place. After some weeks of therapy, though, one day in a trance session his subconscious indicated that it wanted to work in a past life. I duly guided Alan back through time (using a regression technique I call the IMR Regression) and as the trance state deepened he relaxed more and more, his body motionless in the chair, his breathing slow and deep. He remained in this peaceful state for a time as he moved back in his memory banks to retrieve the past life that needed working on. Suddenly, however, he began to move. His body began to shake, and he started to shiver violently. His breathing quickened and his hands started to rub up and down his arms. For a few moments he wrapped his arms around his body as if he was trying to keep warm, as his teeth began chattering and his legs clamped tightly together. It was obvious that he had accessed the past life and his body was remembering the feelings of being there. I asked him where he was:

"I'm outside and it's very cold. I'm moving slowly and I'm alone in a snowstorm."

I asked him if he was male or female and to tell me what he was wearing. Through his shivers he responded:

"I'm a man. I'm wearing heavy, long boots and a thick oilskin. I feel very cold and frightened."

I felt some curiosity about the word 'oilskin' as this felt like a very specific and unlikely piece of information that he had given me. I asked him what the reason was for him being out in a snowstorm. His reply 'rang a bell' with me but I was careful not to suggest anything to him so as not to lead him in any way:

"I feel relief because I feel I've been a burden to the others. There wasn't enough food so I'm helping them by going out to die. I'm trying to save the others."

His breathing continued to sound harsh, coming through chattering teeth, and his arms remained wrapped around his body in an effort to try to keep warm.

"We were in a tent. It's very, very cold. We're all men. We've been there for a few days but we can't move on as the weather's too bad. I know I'm going to die. I tell the others 'I'm just going out - I may be some time'. I leave the tent and walk off. It's so cold. I'm just laid in the snow now. I know I've had it."

Those words - 'I'm just going out, I may be some time' confirmed my suspicions about his identity, but I didn't say anything to Alan, simply allowing him to continue with the experience. Suddenly, he stopped shivering and breathing hard and a smile came over his face as his mood lightened. I asked him what was happening now.

> *"I'm thinking of home. I'm remembering being a child, sitting at home in front of a big, roaring fire. Mother and father are there. It's the family home, back in Selbourne in England. I think it's in Hampshire. I'm remembering being back at school now. It's a boarding school and I'm about 14. It's very strict. I'm happy, quite comfortable and I get on with the other chaps. I'm remembering happier times as I'm dying. Eton was good, those were the good old days. Now, though I'm feeling upset. I'm still quite young and I think my father's died. I go into officer training in the military. I join the army after Eton and I went to Africa. I'm looking forward to an adventure. I think it's the Boer War. It's not nice, very bloody and I can see lots of bodies. The Boers are like madmen. We're taking quite a beating. My men have really suffered. I'm a Captain, leading the chaps into action. I'm terrified but it's exhilarating also. It's hard as we're outnumbered in this battle and we're trying to gain some ground back. We're winning but taking heavy losses. I feel terrible but we've got to follow orders. The war's over and we're back in England. I'm trying to recover. I got my medal and feel proud. I did the best I could."*

Alan began shivering again and his arms moved quickly up and down each other.

> *"I'm back in the snow again and I can feel myself drifting. It's so, so cold and I'm ready to die."*

Slowly, Alan's shaking and frantic movements began to subside, his breathing softening and his body relaxing in the chair. Finally, he lay still and sighed deeply. I asked him what he was experiencing:

"I feel relaxed, warm and safe. It's beautiful and peaceful."

The end had obviously come. I asked him what his name was in that lifetime and immediately, without any hesitation, Alan replied:

"Oates. Lawrence Edward Grace Oates. At Eton the chaps called me Oatey."

I had expected the name Oates, but not the full name which I certainly wasn't aware of. We had a few minutes before the end of the session so I asked him to tell me a little more about the group of men he was with:

"We're going on a big adventure, trying to get to the Pole. It's going to be a bit of race as the Norwegians are trying to get there first. We're led by Scott. He's very definitely in charge. We're still on the boat and it's a long and dangerous journey but we're full of antici- pation as we're a good team. We should be OK. It's a long time to be away but we're OK."

We finished the session and I brought Alan out of hypnosis. He was shocked and dumbfounded by what he had relived. He was particularly amazed at the amount of information he had given, as he was positive he knew very little about the Scott of the Antarctic expedition. We discussed the possibility that he had read a book or seen some documentary or other on TV about the expedition but he was positive that that had never happened. The only thing he felt he might have seen as a boy was the old John Mills movie from the 1940's. I watched this movie a little while later in order to check it out but I can confirm it did not give very much information about Oates. So where had all of that come from? He left the room still confused and bewildered, promising not to do any research at all on the life of Oates before our next session. I too was shocked, especially when I checked in Wikipedia's biography of Oates to find that virtually everything Alan had said was true. His full name *was* Lawrence Edward Grace Oates. He *was* brought up at Selbourne in Hampshire. He *did* go to boarding school and he *was* at Eton when he was 14. His father *did* die when he was only 16. He *did* join the army after leaving Eton and he *did* see action in the Boer War, later becoming a Captain. He *did* join Scott's expedition which was seen as a big adventure, and he *did* view Scott's leadership as authoritarian (*"he's very definitely in charge"*). Ultimately, he *did* sacrifice himself in a vain attempt to give the others a chance of living (this, surely, would be the only thing Alan would have known in advance from any previous knowledge of Oates). So, where *did* all of that come from? The only thing he'd mentioned that might not have been correct is that Oates possibly left the tent not in his boots but wearing only his socks, but that is surely just a minor mistake that should not take away credence from everything else he had got right. Was I looking at the possibility of this shy, gentle man being the reincarnation of one of English history's greatest tragic heroes? As you can imagine, I was looking forward to finding out more.

Chapter 21

More Unknown Facts

Our next session began with Alan expressing his surprise at what had happened, and giving me his word that he had not done any research on Oates or the Scott expedition. After a brief chat I guided him into hypnosis and back into the past life. This time, he went to an earlier time in Oates' life, on board ship with Scott's expedition, on the way to the Antarctic:

"I'm outside, on the deck of a ship, feeding horses. The horses are unsettled, they don't like being at sea. I'm worried they'll get too wet. Evans is going to improve the shelter for them. They're in stalls. I go down below. It's getting cold and I'm getting more excited about what's to come. We're all together checking the kit. Scott's looking at charts. I'm trying to decide which kit to take and which to leave. It's colder than we thought but we need to travel light. We're huddling round the stove to keep warm. I'm on deck now and it's getting much colder. There's much more ice and I don't know how much further the ship can go. There's a lot of noise as the ship breaks the ice but the pace is much slower. I don't think we'll get much further before we have to leave the ship."

Alan paused for a few moments, before moving on:

"We're on the ice now. We've gone as far as we can and we're getting ready to unload. There's just nothingness around, but it's very peaceful. We need to unload as quickly as we can and get a shelter made for winter. Men are hauling the equipment onto the ice so we can move a bit further into the bay for winter. The weather's getting worse so we need to be ready. We've put the horses to work,

pulling the equipment but I'm not sure they're going to be too good. They don't like the snow and it's too cold. They've not travelled too well. They've been reasonably well-fed but they're still malnourished. Evans and some of the other men are on with building a hut for the winter."

Again Alan paused whilst time passed, and then with a smile he continued:

"We're in the hut. It's quite cosy really. There's a big wood burning stove. The days are quite long but we keep ourselves amused."

I asked him how this was done and he laughed gently:

"Dominoes and singing and having quite a jolly time. Someone's got a squeezebox."

After a few moments his smile faded and he became serious again:

"I'm outside and we've had to slaughter some of the ponies. They're not coping well at all. It's a source of fresh meat but I don't like the thought of it. We're nearly ready to start. We've spent winter here and the weather's improved and it's getting lighter."

I asked Alan to move ahead to another significant time, and within a few seconds his body began twisting in the chair, shivering and wrapping his arms around him. His breathing quickened and I asked him where he was. Through chattering teeth he replied:

"I'm inside, in a tent. I'm cold and hungry. We're all hungry. We're stuck, not able to move. The weather's too bad. We're not far from the food dump but the weather's too bad. We only have two days of

fuel and a day's food. We're already on half rations. We've discussed the situation and Evans has said we should share out the morphine tablets. If we can't move soon it will be the better way to go. I'm worse than the others. I think they know it but we don't talk about it. We're all putting on a brave face. I'm very malnourished and severely frost-bitten. I don't have much hope. My feet and fingers are frost-bitten. I can't take my boots off. I'm not scared though, I'm resigned to dying. I feel guilty. If the weather improves the others might make the food dump but I'm slowing them down. We're in the tent, we know the seriousness of our situation. The storm outside is horrendous. We discuss the options. We all receive 30 morphine tablets. There are just four of us left."

SB: "How do you feel about the others?"

"They're brave. It's a great shame we didn't reach the Pole first. We were all upset but we knew for a long time that it wasn't likely we'd get there first. We had far, far too much mechanical equipment. Scott always wanted us to travel lighter, without the ponies or the machines. We had far too much untested equipment. We're making some tea, half a pint of tea. It's very strong and helps us take our minds off the cold for a short while. Scott's writing in his diary. He's writing less and less. He's very tired. We're discussing what we should do. It's decided that we should share out the morphine. We're hoping the weather will improve tomorrow. We're so close but I think we all know it's not likely to happen. Bowers hands out the tablets. I know I can't go on, I'm too weak and too tired. I keep hallucinating, seeing the ponies on the boat. I had to look after the ponies. I've made the decision that they might last another day if they share the rations. I'm a terrible hindrance to them and I'll only slow them down even more. I've got to go outside, they might have a chance with my extra rations. I say a quick goodbye and tell them I'm going outside. They know I'm not coming back, I can see it in their eyes. Not much is said. I wish them luck. Scott shakes my hand. I go out into the snow. I try to get as far away as I can. I've swallowed the tablets. I'm stumbling through the snow. I try to get

*as far away as I can, but I don't think they'll come after me. They
know why I've gone. It's bitterly cold and I'm laid in the snow. I can
feel myself drifting. I'm starting to feel numb. I know I'm dying but
I don't feel any regret. I've lived an adventurous life. I feel numb.
I'm floating up. I feel warm and calm. At peace."*

With those words, spoken quietly as his breathing quietened
down and his body relaxed in the chair, Alan experienced the sad
but honourable death of Oates.

As at the close of our previous session, once Alan came out of
trance he expressed shock at the memories he had relived, and he
wondered how much of it was true. At the time I was unable to
answer him, but having researched Oates death I can once more
confirm that most of it turned out to be true, including Alan
producing some new information that is unknown to historians.

To give you some background information on Scott's Antarctic
expedition, in September 1909 Captain Robert F. Scott announced
the official launch of the British Antarctic Expedition. Shortly
before this two American explorers claimed to have reached the
North Pole, and after Shackleton's failed attempt in that same
year (coming as close as 97 miles of the South Pole) speculation in
Victorian England had reached fever pitch over the possibility of
another expedition to discover the unconquered South Pole.

In 1910 Oates was accepted as a member of Scott's team, with
his role being to look after the ponies (Alan was correct once
more) which were to be used for sledge hauling during the first
half of the trek. Having reached Antarctica, after a long and
perilous sea journey, 16 members of the expedition set off for the
South Pole on 1st November 1911. At various points on the 895
mile journey support members of the team were sent back by
Scott to the base camp until only the 5-man polar party of Scott,
Wilson, Bowers, Evans and Oates remained to walk the last 167
miles to the Pole. On 18th January 1912 they finally reached the
Pole only to discover that Norwegian explorer Roald Amundsen

and his 4-man team had beaten them in the race to be the first there.

Scott and his men faced appalling conditions on the return journey, due to extraordinarily bad weather, inadequate supplies of food, injury and frostbite. Evans died as a result of a fall and Oates feet became severely frost-bitten, making the difficult progress of the surviving 4 men even slower and painful. Day after day the party struggled on, until eventually Oates' frostbite proved to be so severe that he was unable to help the others haul the sledge. With three exhausted men doing the work of four fit men (Oates humiliatingly only able to limp uselessly alongside the sledge whilst his companions desperately pulled for their lives), they barely managed to travel at half the speed they had clocked up on the outward march, and they were now suffering from the effects of much lower temperatures, scurvy, malnutrition and thirst. Temperatures plummeted to minus 43 degrees Fahrenheit and weather conditions worsened as the men desperately fought to reach a food depot that would give them a chance of survival. Oates' condition continued to worsen, and on the 11th March Scott wrote in his Journal:

'Oates is very near the end, one feels. What we or he will do, God only knows. We discussed the matter after breakfast; he is a brave fine fellow and understands the situation, but he practically asked for advice. Nothing could be said but to urge him to march as long as he could.'

As a result of this discussion Scott ordered Wilson (not Bowers as stated by Alan) to hand each man a lethal dose of 30 opium tablets in case they needed to commit suicide should all hope of pulling through be surrendered. Four days later Oates' situation was so desperate (the pain from his gangrene must have been unbearable) that he felt he could not move on any further and asked to be left behind in his sleeping bag to die. The others would not hear of this and urged him to soldier on. He managed a few more miles but his condition worsened and on the morning of the 16th March, in a despairing effort to sacrifice himself so his comrades should have some small chance of survival, he left the tent in which the four men were desperately sheltering from the ravages of an Antarctic storm and staggered through a raging blizzard to his death. Scott's Journal records his final actions:

'Should this be found I want these facts recorded. Oates' last thoughts were of his mother, but immediately before he took pride in thinking that his regiment would be pleased with the bold way in which he met his death. We can testify to his bravery. He has borne his suffering for weeks without complaint and to the very last he was willing to discuss outside subjects. He did not - would not - give up hope till the very end. He was a brave soul. This was the end. He slept through the night before last, hoping not to wake; but he woke up in the morning - yesterday. It was blowing a blizzard. He said 'I am just going outside and may be some time'. He went out into the blizzard and we have not seen him since.

We know that Oates was walking to his death, but though we tried to dissuade him, we know it was the act of a brave man and an Englishman. We all hope to meet the end with a similar spirit and assuredly the end is not far'.

Trapped in their tent by the weather and too weak and malnourished to continue, Scott, Wilson and Bowers eventually died nine days later, only 11 miles short of the food depot. Their frozen bodies were found by a search party on 12th November 1912. Oates' body was never found.

Of course this is a tragic story, the general details of which I expect are known by many people who have an interest in English history, but I wonder how many of us with just an *average* knowledge of Scott's expedition would have been able to provide some of the specific details that Alan did during the session. For example, he correctly stated that there were only four of them left in the tent, and he also correctly gave their names (the others being Scott, Wilson and Bowers). He was right in mentioning his frostbite and malnourished state, and he was also correct in saying that he was in charge of looking after the ponies on the voyage to Antarctica, a journey which caused much suffering to the animals which were indeed kept tethered in stalls on board the ship. Alan was totally accurate in saying that they disembarked in a bay, that they had to work fast (before mid-winter darkness descended) to build a shelter, using the ponies to haul equipment. Alan's concern over the state of the ponies was entirely factual, in that Oates' role initially on the expedition was to look after the animals, which caused Oates much disquietude as they were totally unsuited to the task at hand and the long sea journey had taken its toll on them. He was right in stating that they overwintered there, before they started the trek to the South Pole. He knew that at the end they were trapped in a tent in horrific weather conditions, with a storm blowing outside, and that they had very little food left but that they were close to their objective of a food store. All of these, I feel, are pretty convincing pieces of evidence in terms of acknowledging the probability of Alan truly being Oates' reincarnation. However, the one fact that Alan knew which is even more convincing is that of the poison that the men handed round a few days before Oates died. Few people, other than historians or students of the expedition, would have known they took opium or morphine with them in case (to paraphrase Scott's last diary entry) things came out against them. Although Alan said that they were morphine tablets (they were, in fact, opium tablets) he was absolutely spot on in saying they received 30 tablets each. It is not known if any of the men actually took their lethal dose in order to hasten the end, and some writers and historians think they did not, but Alan was convinced that Oates had taken his as he left the tent to die. All of these facts are quite impressive in supporting my claim for Alan to have been the reincarnation of Oates. Even though he was not totally accurate on a few points (mentioning Evans in the tent when he had, in fact, died four weeks' previously, feeling that they were given morphine tablets rather than opium, and saying that it was Bowers who handed the tablets out rather than Wilson), these are all minor discrepancies which could be explained away by the desperate mental and physical state that Alan was experiencing as he relived the physical feelings of Oates' last days. He did state that he was hallucinating at times, which could account for such small mistakes. To have witnessed Alan in hypnosis as I did, writhing and shivering, his speech broken and clipped as he re-experienced the distress of Oates' wretched last few days (and yet, like Oates, in an uncomplaining and stoical way), is to know that what he was reliving was very real, not just something from his imagination.

POSTSCRIPT

Some time after Alan and I had finished the hypnotherapy together (which, I may say, had a profound effect upon Alan helping him to feel much more confident in himself. His staff at his business all noticed a considerable change in him. He felt more positive, happier and his shyness was transformed into a lovely sense of humour.) I contacted him and asked him to write a little about his thoughts on the therapy he had undergone. He wrote:

> When I was first introduced to "Past Life Regression" it was completely unknown to me. I came to know about it during my sessions, when Steve asked me if there was anything in this life, or a past life, which I would like to talk about.
> During the following sessions I began to recall memories which had caused me pain in my present life, but in later sessions as the therapy continued I started to tell Steve that I had memories of laying in the snow and thinking of my mother. I knew I was dying. I was very cold. (After this session Steve told me I had been visibly

shaking so much so that he had covered me with a blanket.)

Steve asked me if I knew who I was and I replied, "Yes, I am Captain Lawrence Edward Grace Oates".

We continued the sessions for some weeks going back through the earlier memories of the Antarctic Expedition, his army career, and his time at Eton.

The sessions revealed many memories the details of which were not generally known. Some of these have been mentioned in the book.

I have since read, over a year later, a book on Oates' life. I have found some very remarkable, unnervingly similar character traits to my own!!

My experience of Past Life Regression left me initially quite bemused by the whole experience. It was not unpleasant, but has left many unanswered questions in my mind.

Where do these memories come from?

Why were they so intense?

Was I Oates in a previous life???

Chapter 22

I Don't Believe It!

One of the most enjoyable aspects of being a hypnotherapist is that every day is different. Each day in my therapy practice I am treating a variety of issues. One client may come in for help with a phobia, the next person may have a physical illness, the next one suffers from anxiety or depression, and then I might see someone with weight problems. As you can imagine, this helps to prevent staleness which could occur if I was just working with the same things day after day.

One issue which I have often successfully used hypnosis to treat has been that of releasing blocks to learning. These can often occur when someone is trying to revise for an exam and they find that the information they are trying to remember simply won't go into their brains. It can also occur if they are trying to learn a new process such as driving a car or when an actor is attempting to remember lines of text in readiness for a stage appearance. Usually the treatment for it is quite prosaic. However, as you will see, on one occasion treating it for my last client featured here produced utterly unexpected results.

I realise that my final 'character from history' is probably one of the biggest name-drops of all. At first sight, also one of the most unlikely. However, as with all of my clients who regressed spontaneously into famous past lives, this client had no prior in-depth knowledge of his previous incarnation. In fact, I would say that he had no knowledge at all of the historical facts surrounding his former life. This is partly because so little is actually known anyway, and also because my client had never studied the period of history at all.

Terry was a middle-aged retired boxing trainer who had fallen in love with Italy as a result of several holidays there. He had started to learn to speak Italian so he could enjoy his future travels to that country in more depth. However, he was finding it very difficult to keep up with the other people on his Italian night-class and he was struggling to retain knowledge of the language. In his words, 'things get into a muddle'. As well as this, he felt shy and embarrassed in the classroom. He was frightened of asking questions and he admitted to a lack of confidence in himself generally.

When I asked him about his childhood learning experiences he told me that he had never been particularly academic and his time at school was difficult and, at times, traumatic. Firstly, as a child he was naturally left-handed but was forced to write with his right hand. Secondly, he had painful memories of being regularly humiliated by a vicious teacher in front of his class when he was young. Amongst other things the teacher would call him stupid and make him write with a chalk on slate to embarrass him. The same teacher had singled him out and smacked him for misspelling a word with all the other children watching.

No wonder he found learning difficult with all that childhood emotion locked up inside him. Essentially, he would go into 'fear mode' whenever he was in a learning situation because he had experienced such unpleasant times as a lad at school. His mind had come to associate learning with pain and fear. I expected that we would be able to sort out Terry's difficulties in learning Italian quite quickly, primarily by neutralising his early negative school memories. We would then enhance the positive learning resources which I knew he already had inside him but which he was not aware of. However, just in case there were any other deeper, underlying causes to the problem hidden in the subconscious, once Terry was in trance I ensured that we got an Ideo Motor Response so I could check things out. Using this finger response, his subconscious indicated that as well as the Significant Emotional Events in his early life there were also a total of five previous lives which needed to be worked through and neutralised. We began work opening up these past lives in order to release the negative emotions and energies which had been holding Terry back.

Four of the past lives were fairly standard, containing locked-in grief, fear and traumatic death experiences, and as he relived them they were cleared of the negative effects they had had upon him in this present lifetime. One of the lives, however, stood out as it took place in an historically verifiable event from World War II. Although this is not the famous life which is the subject of this book, I include it here as Terry came up with some details which I'm sure he would not have known unless he truly was re-experiencing a former life.

Once in trance in that particular session and having been guided by me back into the past, Terry found himself as a young man in a boiler room on board a ship. He became agitated and I asked him where he was and what he was doing. His reply came quickly:

"I'm in a boiler room, shovelling coal into flames. There's a loud bang and there's water and steam everywhere. I'm running, trying to get out. I climb up two flights of ladders. There's a lot happening, people running everywhere. I can hear explosions. I'm on a ship. I come down a deck under a walkway. We're chopping away life rafts. Everybody's jumping off. I'm in the water - I've jumped. I've swallowed some - it's horrible - salty and oily. She's going over. I've a real bad feeling. It's a warship, a German ship. I feel really sad. I pull myself onto a life raft. Somebody's moaning and shivering in the raft. The ship goes down, the water's grey. Some poor lads are gasping in the water, oiled up. I drag them up. They're saying 'danke, danke'. I can see three rafts. There's lots of debris and oil in the water. I'm alright. I can hear someone shouting 'hindervolt' from the water - don't know if that's my name. It was a big ship, like a battleship. We're roping the three rafts together and paddling away.

The sea's very calm. I can't believe how calm the water is, there are no waves. There are a lot of dead in the water, there was a big explosion. It's all happened so quickly. I think it's World War II. It's cold, somewhere in the North, like Norway or somewhere like that. We're getting picked up by small, fast boats. The name Tirpitz keeps coming."

Terry became silent for a while as he relaxed again. I asked him to move to the next significant time in that life:

"I'm in a dockyard, wearing a German sailor's uniform. I'm at a ceremony, receiving a medal. I'm walking down the docks. It's somewhere up North. I think that's why a lot died, because it was so cold. I think my name was Klaus."

Terry was silent for a while before he continued:

"It's fading now. I feel I'm leaving it and floating out of it."

Terry came out trance, somewhat surprised at what he'd experienced.

After the session Terry did some research and found that the details he gave whilst in trance were factually correct. The German battleship the Tirpitz was sunk on the 12th November 1944 by Lancaster bombers. It was in a bay West of Trimso in Norway. It sank within minutes of being hit and approximately 1000 of its 1700 crew perished. "No wonder" he said, "the water was so calm when the ship went down. There were no waves - we were in a Norwegian fjord." I find it unlikely that Terry would have known these things if he had not, in fact, been reliving a previous life.

I was pleased with the work that Terry and I had done in our sessions together as it was having the required effect. We had released all of the past life traumas and also neutralised his negative childhood learning experiences from this present life. He was finding his Italian classes much easier and he was learning and remembering the new language and showing more skill when speaking it. As well as this he felt more comfortable in himself generally, was more assertive and confident, and he reported that he felt he had lost a negative, depressing feeling which had always dogged him and held him back in life. I taught him self-hypnosis so he could continue strengthening himself by using positive affirmations to empower his subconscious mind. I felt that the therapy process was close to finishing as he had achieved his objective of learning and speaking Italian, and he agreed to come for one final session to consolidate things. Little did I realise that this final session would contain such revelations that we carried on doing many more regressions, opening up the life of one of the most famous people in history.

Chapter 23

Positive Past Life Therapy

A technique I have found to be invaluable in terms of helping clients to enhance skills, abilities and resources, is that of exploring what I call 'Positive Past Lives.' Although most Past Life Therapy involves working in traumatic events in previous lifetimes in order to release negative emotions which are causing present life problems, it is possible to regress back into less painful past lives in order to bring positive energies, abilities and resources into this life. For example, if someone comes to me for help with learning to play a musical instrument it may be possible to regress them into a former life in which they had musical skills. I would then open up those musical energies in the past lifetime and bring those energies and talents back into their present life. I wondered if we could do the same for Terry and when I asked his subconscious using the Ideo Motor Response it indicated there was such a past life. I regressed him back into it in my usual way and gave him a few moments to settle into the life. I then asked him where he was and what he was experiencing:

"I'm outdoors, it's sunset. I'm a man and I'm sitting on a horse, crossing a shallow river. Someone's walking in front of me, leading me. I'm wearing browny-red clothes and a wide-brimmed hat."
SB: "How do you feel?"
"I feel quite well-to-do. I'm coming up to an enclosed town, going across a small low bridge through a town gate. There are chickens and goats around. I get off my horse, swinging my left leg over rather than my right leg. I go into an inn and I can hear Italian but I'm not Italian."

After a pause, during which Terry seemed to be settling into the past life, he continued:

"I'm in a room. There's a bed and a fire. A girl brings in some water and pours it into a bowl. I take my hat off and wash. I think I've got a goatee beard. I go downstairs for something to eat. A man and a woman speak to me. I can communicate but not in their language. I feel as if I'm some sort of traveller. I eat food in a bowl - chicken, and drink white wine from a leather tankard. I'm going up to bed now, with a candle. There are glowing embers in the fire. It's a massive bed with soft pillows.

It's the next morning now. I get back on the horse, from the right again. I'm being led by a man and I'm leaving. I'm overlooking a big bay, looking down over a town with red-roofed houses. It's a busy town with small cobbled streets and dogs wandering around. It feels that this is where I need to be. It's really steep leading down to the sea. I come back later in the day to the inn and I'm back in my room, standing at a window looking down to the bay. I sit and write into a big book. It's English, very fine writing and it's like a diary.

It's night now and I'm sitting by the window, smoking a long, white clay pipe. I feel really relaxed. I'm some sort of writer, maybe a playwright. I think it's the 16th Century."

We were coming to the end of the session and so I asked Terry if he could become aware of the name of the person. A part of me wondered if he might have been someone relatively famous, maybe a minor Elizabethan playwright or something. Terry went quiet for a while, and started to shake his head. I wasn't sure if he was finding it difficult to hear or sense his name. Then he said:

"No, no, I can't believe it. I can't believe the name I'm getting Steve. It's too fantastic."

I insisted he give me the name. He breathed deeply and said:

"It's Will. My name is Will. William Shakespeare."

I brought Terry out of trance and we both sat looking at each other, astonished and incredulous at what had come through. We discussed things and were both sceptical as to the reality of what he'd experienced. However, we were also fascinated and keen to explore things further so Terry agreed to do another session, with a strong warning from me not to look at anything remotely Shakespearian in between times. Thus began an intriguing journey for both of us, throwing up surprises and possibilities each time we regressed back into the life.

Chapter 24

Glimpses of Shakespeare

Terry returned the following week and after a short discussion, during which we agreed not to pre-judge anything but just to go along with whatever Terry saw or sensed whilst in trance. I hypnotised him and guided him back into the past life which had dropped upon us like a bombshell. After a long pause, whilst he began to make sense of the images he was getting in his mind's eye, Terry began to speak softly:

> *"I'm walking through an archway by a river. It's daytime and I'm in a town on my own. There's a stone bridge. I go into a house through a big wooden door with massive hinges. The walls are four or five bricks thick. I go down a couple of steps into a room which has flag stones on the floor. There's a table with candles on it and a fireplace which has long, thin red bricks around it. There's a pan on an open fire - it's a big, black bowl. I get something to eat. I feel fit and well and I think I'm about 30. I carry a white-handled sword on my right side. I've just moved it out of the way to sit at the table. I'm eating a bowl of broth. There's a woman sitting sowing or something. I think she might be connected to me. Her name's Francis. Once I've eaten I sit quietly by the fire, reading and smoking a pipe. I can see the word 'orange' written on the top left-hand corner of the book."*

I asked Terry to become aware of the type of work he did in that life. Without a pause he replied:

> *"I'm a writer. I feel happy with plenty of energy for it. I'm smoking my pipe whilst I'm doing it. I'm writing with my left hand on single bits of paper, out of the big book I had in Italy."*

I asked Terry to move to another scene from the life, and he saw himself outdoors:

"I'm in a market square in England. I'm talking to some people, showing them the papers I've written. They're actors, but we're not in a theatre. They smile wryly, in approval. They've cleared an area and people are gathering round. There's a hay cart nearby. There's a sort of play going on. The man who's taking charge is called George. The audience is talking. People are stood up. There's funny banter with the audience. The performance is on the street, and I've written what they're performing. George sticks out all the time. He's wearing a big, false nose. It's finished and people are walking away laughing. The actors are enjoying it. They all give me the pieces of paper back - they've been reading from them whilst performing. It's been a rehearsal. I go back to the house and Francis greets me. I'm happy because it's gone well. She's a lot older than me, but she's not my wife.

I've packed up my stuff and my papers and I'm in a carriage going to London. I feel I've tried something out and I'm going to London to push it. The words Comedy of Errors comes to mind, but I don't know why."

I asked Terry to take his time and become aware of his name in the life. He spent a couple of minutes in silence, during which he seemed to be considering words which he was hearing in his head. Eventually he spoke:

"It's William. William Shakespeare. That's the name that keeps coming to me Steve."

As time was up I brought Terry out of hypnosis. As you can imagine, we were both amazed again by the memories he had relived. Prior to the session I had half expected him to struggle to come up with anything tangible, particularly as he was so unacademic that he would possibly have found it difficult to even spell the word Shakespeare correctly. If that had happened, and his attempts to relive the past life had proved fruitless, it would have suggested that our previous session was little more than fantasy. However, quite the opposite had happened. He had provided information which could fit into the life of an actor-playwright. The idea of Shakespeare trying out scenes from a play, outdoors in a town or village, in order to gauge audience reaction prior to putting it on in a London theatre, is entirely plausible. This would especially be the case if he was still in the early phase of his career as a playwright. Once he had achieved fame and status as a writer he would not need to resort to such a plan, as his proven track record would have ensured his plays would have been rehearsed and performed in a theatre. Surely, if Terry had been making things up, trying to prove that he was Shakespeare, he would have been unlikely to have come up with something as odd as the young playwright trying out scenes from a work-in-progress in the middle of a market place.

Terry felt that at this stage of the life he was about 30 years of age. As Shakespeare was born in 1564 this would mean that the scene he had witnessed was maybe in the early 1590's. Just before the end of the session he mentioned the play Comedy of Errors, which is interesting in that, although accurate dating of most of Shakespeare's plays is said to be notoriously difficult, some scholars believe Comedy of Errors to belong to his earliest period which began in the early 1590's. Bearing in mind that Terry had never studied the period or even read any plays by Shakespeare in his life (indeed, he told me that whilst at school he would have shied away from such things), this does seem to be quite a coincidence. I began to wonder if I really was doing Past Life Regression with the reincarnation of the greatest writer in the English language.

Chapter 25

Putting Flesh on the Bones

So began a whole series of meetings with Terry extending over several months. Throughout this process Terry did no reading or studying of Shakespeare. He conscientiously stayed away from anything remotely Shakespearian or Elizabethan so that he could not confabulate anything he had seen or read into our sessions. I too did not lead him in any way, at all times when he was in trance making him produce memories himself. Although this was at times a slow process, it meant that everything he experienced was 'clean' and came only from him. Nothing was implanted by me during our sessions.

In his regressions he came up with all sorts of detail which I think puts flesh on the bones of what is actually known about Shakespeare. Given that there have been so many hundreds (if not thousands) of biographies of him over the centuries, people with no knowledge of the period are often surprised to learn that the amount of detail that is factually known about Shakespeare could be written on the back of a postcard. All of those countless biographies are filled with conjecture but in truth very little really is known about one of the most famous figures in history.

During our time together Terry reported an array of information which fits in very well with what is known or hypothesised about Shakespeare. At no time did he produce anything which appeared to be fantasy, unreal or anachronistic. All this from someone who left school at 15 with no qualifications and no desire to succeed academically.

In our next regression, once in trance Terry opened up memories of a man who appeared several times in our sessions and who seems to have been important in terms of helping

Shakespeare to get his plays performed. As usual, I began by asking him where he was:

> *"I'm in a coach, clattering across a big wooden bridge across a big river. The bridge has got buildings on it and it feels like it's covered over, not open. I can smell smoke everywhere. We come off the bridge and bear right. It's London. We go along a track to a big house with trees around it. I'm being welcomed there as a visitor. I go into a big room with a big table and high-backed chairs. I'm asked if I've brought much work. The work that I've brought is in big, soft, leather-bound folders. It's written work. A man's looking at the work, he's about 50 years old. I feel a lot younger than him, maybe about 28. I've come to him for an opinion or a judgement on the work and I'm looking on expectantly. I think he's important for the plays. He's looking through one piece of work but there are about five altogether. I can see the writing but I can't make out what it says. He's just moved by the fire and he's said something like 'this work will be seen'. He's somebody who I'm seeing for advice and comments. He's well known, one of the top men, maybe in acting or production. I'm staying here and I'm being taken to my room. Now I'm laid in the bed feeling really good."*

Just as an aside, but which again suggests that what Terry was seeing was true, the old London Bridge which he appears to have crossed did indeed have buildings on it. We are accustomed nowadays to think of the current London Bridge which was built in Victorian times. The medieval bridge which Shakespeare would have crossed was constructed over 33 years and opened during the reign of King John in 1209. John licensed the building of houses on it as a means of deriving revenue for its mainte-nance, many of which soon became shops. Contemporary pictures show it crowded with buildings (some of them seven stories high) on either side of the bridge, reducing the road for traffic (horses, carts, wagons and pedestrians) to a narrow passageway. Nearly 200 businesses lined both sides of the constricted street, with many of the top floors of the buildings built over the street and actually connected to the house or shop across from them. Terry's statement that it felt covered-in was actually the case, as in parts it would have resembled a tunnel. I find it hard to believe that Terry would have known this prior to our sessions, something which is only usually known to students of history.

A few weeks later in other regressions Terry again had contact with the same man. This time, we got a bit closer to his significance:

"I've been travelling. I've got a big trunk with my belongings in it and I'm on a quayside, going on board a ship. I've been away for some time."

Terry was quiet for a short time, as if experiencing the passing of time in the past life, before he spoke again:

"I'm across in London now. We've docked along the South Bank of the Thames. I travel in a coach and go past the bridge with buildings on it. We're going further and further on before we go across another, smaller bridge. We're heading north, through a heavily wooded area. It has oak trees growing and lots of old trees. We've gone a long way and eventually we stop at Banbury. It's night-time. We've gone under an archway into the courtyard of an inn, and my trunk is staying on the carriage. I feel that I'm travelling west for an important meeting with somebody. Somewhere around Oxford. I'm at a big house in the country now and the soft, leather-bound diary books are getting unloaded. The house has a big entrance. The diaries are staying at this house - they're on a massive table. The man's here - I think he's sponsored my travel. The name Charles Worthy comes to mind. Another place just came to me - Nuneaton. Like there's a college there. I feel like I'm going to give a lecture

there. I also feel I'll give another lecture at a place called Stalybridge. Travelling is involved, but I feel they're both in the same region."
SB: "What's your connection with the man, if any?"
"We're working together in some way. He's older than me. It's about plays - there's already some work done in the diaries. He's very well-to-do. It's somewhere between Oxford and Gloucester. Gloucester keeps coming to mind. I'm working with him to put the plays on. Perhaps he's got a theatre? He's the same person I spoke to before when I went south of the Thames - he's got a house there. I'm getting memories of being outside a civic building, maybe a Guildhall or a Town Hall. I seem to be well known in Gloucester to some well-off people, as if they're sponsoring me. Charles Worthy has something to do with these people and he lives east of Gloucester, possibly 30-40 miles away. He has lots of land and a big house. I feel I know the area well. My connection with the man arose on my previous journey down to London, over the bridge and along to the South East, not far from the River Thames. That's where I first took some stuff for him to look at. I think he has a lot of influence in the London theatres. He has a house there, but his main place is across the river, further up travelling north-west. It's a big mansion. It's as if he has the say over what goes on in the theatres. I don't have much time to be at my home because of my work, which feels important. I need to be at this mansion."

In another session, Terry had further dealings with Charles Worthy:

"I've moved to another time at the big house. I'm outdoors on a big terraced area at the back of the house. It's a bluey-grey and white building with lots of glass-tall windows. There are steps down onto gardens and big trees. Lush green grass and then some scrub with beaters working the scrub. We're hunting with birds, falcons. The falcons are killing other birds in mid-air. We walk to where the birds have brought the prey down, give them a piece of meat and take it.

This is Charles Worthy's house. He's like a backer, but he's also a friend and mentor. He's the link between the top people in the theatre and the top people who go to the theatre. He's got a lot of clout. He's pretty robust, but older than me. I'm maybe in my early thirties. He has a massive aviary where he keeps the birds. I feel comfortable here, because I've been here a few times before."

So just who is this mystery man who cropped up several times in our sessions and who appears to have been a very important figure in Shakespeare's life? Is he, as Terry guessed, a rich man who acted as backer for Shakespeare's productions? Or is he relevant in some other way?

Historians and literary writers do not mention such a person in their work. Could it be that the man, Charles Worthy (or possibly his surname Charlesworthy?), had a major role to play in the creation of Shakespeare's plays, giving the young writer advice on the storylines he had collected on his travels abroad? Or could it be that the man was rich enough and influential enough to ensure that the new plays of an up-and-coming playwright received financial backing to guarantee their first productions? He appears to have had a country estate in Gloucestershire and a home south of the Thames where he welcomed Shakespeare as a friend and intimate.

Other possible (and much more controversial) theories regarding his identity are that he might have been collaborating with Shakespeare during the writing of the plays, or that it was he who wrote the plays once Shakespeare had furnished him with ideas and stories he had collected on his travels. As you may know there is a school of thought that Shakespeare was not the author of the plays but that they are written by someone with a more aristocratic background. Some years ago I read a few books on this subject and I was impressed by the arguments and the claims that someone other than Shakespeare wrote the plays. Whenever Terry mentioned the 'mystery man' whilst in trance a part of me wondered if he was receiving storylines or ideas for plays from Shakespeare in order to create the works himself. However, my need to remain impartial meant I was unable to mention this to Terry for fear of implanting something into his mind which could lead him to invent memories which were not real. Frustrating, I know, but I had to let him find out for himself. Unfortunately, we couldn't get a definitive answer. Charles Worthy, whoever or whatever he was, had to remain a mystery. There were more to come.

Chapter 26

The Travels of Shakespeare

Having been introduced to the possibility of Terry being the reincarnation of Shakespeare, we then proceeded to explore many facets of his life. One of the most interesting aspects of the unknown life of Shakespeare were the sessions in which Terry experienced himself as the young writer travelling around Europe. After the shock of the first session in which Terry found himself travelling around Italy, one of the earliest was the following:

SB: "What's happening now?"

"I'm on a ship going out on the River Thames. I'm alone on the upper deck, although I think I have a cabin. It's daytime and I'm going on a long trip. I'm going across the Channel but not to France. I can't go there for some reason but I don't know why. I'm on another boat now from Antwerp, out at sea on the way to Portugal. We go into Lisbon, then somewhere like Tangiers or North Africa. We're loading on loads of ornate carpets. I'm just a passenger."

SB: "What's the reason for your travelling?"

"It's to do with my work. I'm learning. I've got a letter of introduction and we go via Genoa. I'm on the dockside, getting loaded off. I've got two massive wooden boxes of stuff. I'm going to a place of learning, that's what the letter's for. I'm in a coach, alone, going across a viaduct across a valley. Going to Sienna. It feels like I'm in the middle or northern part of Italy. I feel excited. We follow a long winding road before I get to Sienna. We arrive at a college or something like that - it doesn't stand out on its own but it's part of something. Somebody gets my big chests off the coach. I feel I'm in

my early twenties. It's a quiet place. Plenty of people have got skull caps on. I'm indoors now. It's more like a vault than a room, it's all arches. It seems like I've got a lot of freedom and I can go anywhere I want. I'm watching a man writing, he's like a scribe. He's got lovely, scrolling writing. This place is a community, like a monastery. The building is big and it's part of the town, in that the outside of it is the wall of the town. I'm walking around the room, the vault, just observing. It's light, warm and airy, like a colonnade in a courtyard. I'm having a meal now. I'm in a hall with a lot of men who are all dressed the same, wearing reddy-brown cloth and something like a smock. I'm in tights and a shirt. Eating thick, dry bread, cheese and grapes. They're talking to me and I'm sort of responding but I don't really understand what's being said. I'm passing through here but I'm also learning things, watching somebody writing, watching their routine every day, how they busy themselves. I stay maybe a month but I'm leaving now. I will be coming back there as I leave my chest there. I take some clothes with me and I have a bag on my back. I'm on horseback, heading northeast. My companion is a young fellow, younger than me. He's about 17 and the name Giuseppe keeps coming to mind. He's an apprentice from where we've just been and he's leading me. He's going to be a teacher. We're going somewhere else."

After the session, Terry told me that he thought he had been staying in a monastery, observing the daily life of the monks, perhaps with a view of writing about it.

In another regression session Shakespeare's affection for Italy came through strongly:

"I feel as if I'm travelling, maybe to Bologna. I see an L-shaped building with a colonnade around it. It's a dusty red colour. I've just been introduced to someone and shown into a small, narrow room, which is a bit like a cell but more comfortable... Now I'm sitting at a table having a meal. It's very clean and formal. The head person is

sitting on my right and there are a few others at the table. They're well-to-do people and it's a formal welcome for me, perhaps by a guild or something. We have finger bowls and clean cloths to wipe our hands...I've moved on now and I'm on horseback out in the Italian countryside, having a look around. I go into the town and walk around, seeing allsorts going on. There's a market place with straw, carts, horses and donkeys. I've seen so many things and I can feel a really strong urge to write. I can feel it inside me right now. I go back to my room, the small room I saw earlier, and open up the covers of the soft, leather bound book. The date 1584 keeps coming to me and I think I've written it down. I feel I'm in my early twenties. I've got stacks of energy and I'm writing about things I've seen and characters I've met on my travels. The name Dante keeps coming up. The urge to write is really strong. Words keep coming into my mind - 'I doth learneth many truths from thee' and 'my heart hath warmest to thy ways'. I'm feeling very emotional, Steve. I'm writing about the place and putting my feelings for the country down, like it's a diary. I feel a great love for Italy. Can I just rest for a few moments please Steve, I'm feeling really emotional?"

Terry's lip quivered and he took several long, quavering breaths. I allowed him time to compose himself and after a couple of minutes he continued:

"I'm outdoors now, watching a man painting. He's in an open space inside the colonnade and we're looking at a hilly and green landscape. The L-shaped building is probably half of the whole of the building, with an open entrance gate at the other end. It's an important building in the middle of the city. I'm definitely in Bologna. Words keep coming to my mind - 'dost thou knowest Umbria?' and 'of things thy heart might hold'. I think I'm in this place for a while, resting and doing plenty of writing. Sometimes I'm in my room and sometimes in the colonnade. I can see lines I'm writing on the page but they're too vague for me to make out. I feel I'm working on a play."

Unfortunately, we were unable to get a sense of the play he was writing as the images were too vague. As far as I can tell from the information provided by Terry in our sessions, Shakespeare's travels appear to have occurred during two periods of his life. His earlier journeys seem to have taken place when he was in his early twenties, whilst the later ones probably happened in his early to mid-thirties.

A further tantalising snippet from the early period came when Terry briefly saw himself in Spain:

"I can see a big house with three floors and windows like arches. It has a large ornamental lake in the front. It's sunset. A man with black hair is sitting at an easel painting. He's painting dark, snow-capped mountains in the background. I think I'm visiting this man who's an artist. We're in the middle of dry grass. Another man has a glove on and is carrying an eagle on it. It's warm and the sky has an orange glow but it doesn't feel like Italy. The house is made from white or light coloured brick with a red tiled roof. I'm in Spain, it's definitely Spanish."

Shakespeare's peregrinations around Europe in search of ideas for his writing continued in another session:

"I'm outdoors and it's daytime, standing in an open doorway which leads onto a big cobbled stone path. It's like an old temple with columns everywhere. It's very warm and the landscape's dry but green. Way down below, in the distance, is the sea. The land juts out to the left and right, like a horseshoe with the sea in the middle, but it's miles across. I'm on a plateau and walking through old ruins with 3 sets of columns. The columns come from a big building behind me with archways. This was an important place and the names Zeus and Plato come to mind. It's rocky with big boulders around. There have been tremors or earthquakes but the people here don't call them earthquakes. At the back are dark, cool rooms. I think

I'm in Greece. The date 1580-something comes to mind. I can see an Eastern-style carpet hanging up with vivid colours on it. It's a deep, royal blue with a yellow sun on it. The bottom right-hand corner is red, like a desert and the sun's rays are bent, spiralled into the top left-hand corner. There are olive groves and other buildings around as if it's been a settlement and lots of rubble everywhere. I've gone to a market by the harbour now. There's lots of square brickwork and I'm struck by how little wood there is in the buildings. I'm travelling alone and I go to the room where I'm staying. I can see out onto the harbour - it's a big port. Most of the ships have just one mast and one sail. I've still got my big, soft leather-bound books, one of them is on the table. The ink is made up by crushing some beetles with a pestle and mortar and adding spirit." Terry remained quiet for a while and then began: *"I've moved to another day and I'm outside in a marble pagoda-type building with a domed roof at the top of a hill. It's not very big; it's a shaded viewing area. To the left as I look out I can see bluey-green tree-covered mountains. It's very steep and mountainous. It's Greece, Eastern Greece. People are showing me things and they feel insulted that I want to travel east into Turkey so it's as if I'm not allowed to go there. I'm on a ship now and the weather and the sea are rough - I feel rough. I'm travelling alone again, eating rice with black olives and fish. The ship has been into Turkey, and is carrying carpets and cloth from Istanbul. I'm travelling North-west and the weather's calmer now. It's giving me time to write all about where I've been. I'm going back to Venice. I came from there and went down into Greece to see a few ancient sites there. I wanted to go further east but that was upsetting the people there. I go to Venice and then I go to Remagen - I think that's in Germany? I'm walking up the cobbled street. The village overlooks the river to my left. I'm talking to two men in a tavern about my leather-bound book. I'm explaining about my diary, that the ideas for every foreign play are born from this book. Also in the diary are stage settings - drawings of scenery and stuff to accompany the plays."*

Could it be that the young Shakespeare visited all these places looking for inspiration? As a footnote to the above, it should be noted that although dates are sometimes difficult to get right in Past Life Regressions, Terry did feel that the date was 1584 and that he was close to 20 during his Italian and Greek travels. This does tally with reality, in that Shakespeare was born in 1564. Yet another unlikely coincidence for Terry to have got this right. Also, how would Terry have known that ink was indeed made from crushed beetles, a minor fact but one which again suggests he was not making things up? I wonder how Shakespeare managed financially (or was he supported by his rich 'backer' or co-writer Charles Worthy)? For me one of the biggest mysteries, if Terry's Shakespeare memories are true, is about the fate of his travel diaries, those big leather-bound books of parchment he often mentioned. In the same way that there are no surviving manuscripts of any of Shakespeare's works, what an incredible loss to the world of literature that the diaries, if they existed, have not survived the passage of time.

Chapter 27

More Foreign Excursions

In other sessions Terry appeared to be in Shakespeare's early to mid-thirties when he was abroad again, this time possibly either writing plays or looking for material for them whilst sojourning in various foreign places. Once more, Terry provided details which could fit with what is factually known or conjectured about Shakespeare's life. We began again in Italy, on a journey into Germany:

"I'm travelling north-east from Bologna on horseback. I'm not alone, someone's with me. We go towards a big lake near some mountains and then onto an old town with lots of trees and forests around. It's called Remagen. It has something to do with the Romans. It's near a border and it's like an old Roman garrison. I feel I need to know about it - I'm learning about how the Romans lived here. It's a really interesting place and I've got stacks to write about. There are loads of pine trees, statues and flowing water. The buildings are light brown, rounded and the roofs are cone-shaped but not tiled. They're roofed with bricks of stone. It's very hilly before it goes down and becomes flat."

SB: "Approximately how old are you?"

"I'm in my thirties. I feel really interested in everything here. I'm staying here to do some writing. I'm in a big room. There are smaller, thatched houses that have individual patterns on the thatches. Some are tied with cord round part of the thatch, others are flat and overlapped. Some have a square and some have oval trimming at the bottom. The village has a strong tie with ancient Rome but it's also a place in its own right. I think I'm writing a play here. Hamlet. I feel really strong that it was written here."

Terry paused for a couple of minutes, as if experiencing the passage of time, before he went on:

"I'm moving on now, heading towards a seaport, to Antwerp. It's flat and green where I'm going. There's somewhere else I must go, near the coast, to a flat-land on the other side of the mountains. There's a river or a canal. I feel like I'm in Ghent. There's a building here with a fantastic pattern done in a mosaic, near a canal and an open space. I'm walking, sightseeing, but I've come to see this place. It's like a merchant's building, like a covered market. It's massive, an ornate brick or stone building with columns on each side. I go inside and it's like a purpose-built place where people go and sell their wares - cloth, seeds, oil. It's a place where deals are made between merchants. The stuff on show is for bulk buying and cargo. It's a big place, cool, and the noise echoes. The columns are wide enough apart to drive carts in between. This is what I've come to see. I'm looking for inspiration. It could be that I get the inspiration here to write The Merchant of Venice. All the time I've been seeing this I've also had an image in my mind of King Henry VIII and Queen Elizabeth. I have an image in my mind of a crowd of people, including the Queen, coming towards a theatre."

Again, Terry remained silent, before continuing:

"I'm travelling on horseback again, out of Bologna, going north-east again. There are a few of us with lots of gear - bundles and bags. We're taking it nice and easy. I'm singing. I feel really happy. We're like a travelling troupe of actors, going into the North-East of Italy. In the distance on our left I can see a big lake. I feel as if we're going somewhere between the lakes and Venice. We're putting on a show in a market-place. It's a free show for anyone who wants to be there. It's a really funny play, with lots of expression and movement rather than lots of words. I'm taking part in it as well as directing it. There's lots of improvisation and things going on. There are no

seats, just a casual audience with people standing. It's all at a fast pace, actors rushing around and a lot of colour, lots of pennants hanging and we're wearing coloured tassels. It feels like we're in a city or large town."

Terry sighed and moved on to another scene:

"It's daylight and I'm in a big amphitheatre. There's a lot of stone but also a lot of wooden construction around the place. There are wooden rails for the audience to lean on and it's open to the elements. There's an audience and I'm taking part in the perfor-mance, but it's a different play to the last one. It feels like it's a dramatic play. Some of them are dressed as Roman soldiers. I think it's about Julius Caesar. I'm playing a part but I'm also directing things. The audience is sophisticated, members of the gentry. I'm in my mid-thirties, about 37. The play is in several acts, and somebody is explaining each act to the audience before each act is played so that they can keep up with it."

SB: "How did you get involved with these actors?"

"I got involved with them in Bologna. I'd eat and drink with them, they're like-minded people. I feel this play is my work and I think it's in Latin. Some of these players have translated it. It's night-time now and I'm in the amphitheatre, alone. They must have cold nights because all of my body feels really cold. I've got a bad bout of cold and I'm wrapped up by a fire, shivering. I think we're somewhere between the mountains and the sea."

Terry was pleased to finish the session there as his body was shivering in the chair as he recalled this.

The thought of William Shakespeare being involved with what may have been an itinerant group of actors in Italy is a fascinating one, though as with his experience in an earlier session when he felt he was performing in an English market-place, highly plausible. Companies of touring actors and performers roved extensively at that time, both at home and abroad. The pre-eminent acting troupe of the time, The Queen's Men (whom some scholars feel probably admitted the young Shakespeare to their ranks), are recorded as roaming as far from London and Elizabeth I's court as Lancashire in 1588 and Carlisle in 1589. Terry's feelings of intense happiness during the outdoor performance (which was apparent from the big smile he had on his face whilst in trance) bring with them a vivid sense of adventure and joy which must have been in Shakespeare's character. If, as seems likely, they were performing Julius Caesar, then once more Terry appears to have got his dates about right. Shakespeare wrote his tragedy in 1599 (and he did mention that it felt 'a dramatic play') when he was about thirty-five, close to Terry's feeling of being in his mid-thirties.

Could Shakespeare have written Hamlet in Remagen? As we shall see, in other sessions Terry continued to reiterate this. Firstly, however, we join him again in his beloved Italy:

"I'm in a carriage and it's a very bumpy ride. There's only one other person in the carriage. I feel that I'm coming from Verona and going across mountain passes. I feel a really strong pull to Genoa, as if I have to go there...I'm looking down into Genoa and I can see tall-masted, wooden ships and stacks of rigging. The harbour's packed out with ships. The person with me is taking me to the dockside. He's younger than me - I'm about in my mid-thirties, he's in his early twenties, and it's as if he has something to show me. It's a big port, full of ships anchored alongside big wooden jetties. I'm on the wharf-sides and people are telling me stories. They're sea people talking about things that have happened at sea. They're talking and he's translating. There's been a big storm and plenty of damage, that's why there are so many ships in. There's lots of broken rigging and broken masts with no sails. There are lots of excited people. It's something that's not happened for years - the storm. Everywhere you look there are ships that have taken a battering. I'm hearing

stories about how bad it's been. The man with me is excitedly dragging me around to meet different people. There are women crying and youngsters looking up at the ships. It's very busy and people are upset because of the damage to the ships and the loss of life...one ship's rigging is half on the wharf and we have to climb over it to go up the wharf. There are big, thick ropes that have been ripped apart."

Throughout this Terry's voice was serious and sombre. He was obviously moved by the suffering he was witnessing. He paused for a while as if to compose himself, before moving on to another scene:

"I'm writing in my journal - the big leather book-again. It has thick paper, about the full length of my forearm and about the same width for each page. I'm in a room, high up overlooking the port. I can see people working down there by lamplight. It's been an absolutely terrible thing that's happened. The date February 1601 has just come into my mind. The man who's been with me has come into my room, telling me that one hundred ships have come into the harbour, all damaged. Many people have died. I sit writing about it."
SB: "How do you feel?"
"Not as bad as I did on the harbour-side. I felt really emotional."

Terry let out a big sigh, as if releasing some of the feelings he had experienced, and was quiet for some time. When he spoke again he was calmer and it was obvious he had moved on again:

"I'm seeing an old fountain, like a natural spring with clean water running into a round trough. I'm high up in the hills, in a small village, having a drink. It's very hot. I can see the sea. There are two of us. I'm with the man again and we're sitting on the edge of the round trough. The horses are drinking too. A continuous flow of water's trickling out of an ornamental stone onto a tray and into the

trough. I think I'm halfway between Verona and Venice, on my way to Venice. We put the horses under a colonnade. The sun's high and it's very hot, too hot to travel. The village is very quiet and I can see a haze on the sea in the distance. I sense a strong connection between Venice and Remagen. As if my journey begins or ends there. Something to do with my writing. I think as if there's an old trade route, maybe a Roman trade route, between Remagen and Venice. In Remagen I can see Roman ruins. I'm looking at a big mosaic on the floor, with lots of colours - blue, brown and white - and shapes of fishes. The building it's in faces down to the river. I feel I have lots of important writing to do. I'm becoming more and more aware that Hamlet was written here. I definitely wrote Hamlet here. It's an old town with spiral house tops. I'm on the south side of the town on the edge of a wooded area, looking down towards a river. I'm outdoors, writing. A woman brings me a cold drink, I think it's beer. I'm sitting near some rocks with my journal resting on a board like an easel. I feel busy. I'm near a cottage overlooking the river. There's bluey-grey granite rock and bright green grass. The air's clean, so no flies land in the ink. I've got a real flow in the writing and it's coming really easy. After a page of writing I don't have to wait for long for the ink to dry to turn the page over as it's warm outside...I've walked back to the village now and I'm in a tavern where I'm staying talking to some locals. They're asking me where I'm from so I draw a map to show them. They've never heard of it as it's beyond the mountains. They're quite well off, tradesmen I think. They're friendly. One's a tanner and he's amazed I can make money by writing."

On that somewhat prosaic note the session ended. It's those small details that come up in regression sessions that so often suggests to me that my clients really are experiencing their former lives.

Could it really be that William Shakespeare really did travel widely in his twenties and thirties, gleaning ideas for plays which he either wrote whilst abroad or on his return to England? As I've already stated, so little is actually known about his life and what little is known does not provide any details about any travels. However, in my subsequent research for this book I was quite shocked to find information which may support Terry's discoveries. It appears that the first references to the possibility of Shakespeare having travelled in Italy date to as far back as 1838, when writer and traveller Charles Armitage Brown argued that from internal evidence of the plays he must have done so. His chapter entitled 'Did He Visit Italy?' in his book Shakespeare's Autobiographical Poems was followed later in the nineteenth century by the German Shakespearian Karl Elze theorizing that in 1593 Shakespeare 'fled from the dangerous and pestilential atmosphere of the metropolis' and immediately upon his return written The Merchant of Venice and The Taming of the Shrew 'when he was still filled with the impressions he had received, and when the whole charm of Italy and its sky unconsciously guided his pen' (Essays on Shakespeare Translated L. Dora Schmitz 1874, chapter entitled 'The Supposed Travels of Shakespeare). Elze concludes that Shakespeare had spent time at Mantua. In his book 'Notes and Essays on Shakespeare', written in the 1870's, John Wesley Hall reviews Karl Elze's suppositions and has the following to say: 'Dr Elze may be said to add something to the *probability* [my italics] of Shakespeare having visited Italy. It is indeed difficult to believe that the poet never himself saw those fair blue skies beneath which so many of his creations move as beneath their native and proper canopy. Does any non-Italian work transport us into the bright, careless, star-clear South, as the last act of The Merchant of Venice transports us?' Still other writers have written of the likelihood of Shakespeare wandering on the Continent, suggesting that he explored the inland waterways of Northern Italy, finding his way to the Venetian Republic. One writer even advocated the possibility that Shakespeare had joined a company of English comedians in Germany, and as we have seen Terry did relive something of a similar nature as a member of a troupe of roving players in Italy.

More recently, the 2008 book 'Shakespeare in Venice', written by Venice University lecturer Shaul Bassi and writer Alberto Toso Fei, argues that Shakespeare's knowledge and insights about Venice have such a 'local feel' that he must have gained them at first hand (rather than the generally accepted view that he both read widely and that he gleaned information from Italian merchants working in London). He is also thought to have had a working knowledge of Italian.

Plague struck London in 1592-4 and again in 1603, forcing playhouses to close down. It is estimated that 10% of the populace of London died in the plague in 1592 alone. It does make sense to imagine the playwright deserting the pestilential city, returning to write works influenced by his travels. A substantial number of Shakespeare's plays (approximately one third) are set in Italy or make specific references to events and locations in Italy, some including details of Italy probably only known to one who has travelled there, indicating the strong possibility that Terry's memories were real. Terry also relived Shakespeare in Italy at two separate times in Shakespeare's life, around about his twentieth and thirtieth years, which does correspond to the plague years in Elizabethan London. Once more, I find it hard to believe that Terry could have known such things, information which is known only by scholars of the life and works of The Bard, or that he would have made up such highly probable details simply by chance.

As well as this conjecture, which may not be factual evidence but which is hard to dispute, several other pieces of Terry's information seem to be correct. During the sessions in which he was journeying abroad in his thirties, Terry mentioned the writing of three plays: The Merchant of Venice, Julius Caesar and Hamlet, and although the dating of most of Shakespeare's plays is fraught with difficulty, scholars do seem to agree that his work falls into four periods in his writing career. Until the mid-1590's he wrote mainly comedies influenced by Roman and Italian models. His second period began in about 1595 with the tragedy Romeo and Juliet and ended with the tragedy of Julius Caesar in 1599. From around 1600 to about 1608 he wrote mainly tragedies, including Hamlet, and from about 1608 to 1613 mainly tragicomedies or romances. Shakespeare was born in 1564 so he would have been in his early to mid-thirties in the mid-to-late 1590's, which is where scholars place The Merchant of Venice and Julius Caesar. It is not outside the bounds of possibility that Hamlet was written at this time too. If this is correct, then one must wonder how Terry could have known this, never having studied Shakespeare's life or works in any way. At no time during his regressions did he come up with any information which was obviously untrue, anachronistic or impossible to place within what is known or posited about the life of Shakespeare.

One other detail sticks out, which again neither Terry nor I knew until after our sessions, when Terry researched it himself and found it to be true. Remagan was indeed a Roman fortress, and is renowned for its Roman ruins. The more I look at it, the more the likelihood of him being the reincarnation of Shakespeare seems likely.

Chapter 28

A Selection of Titbits

Having explored Terry's travels as Shakespeare, I'd now like to cover a few perhaps minor pieces of information which he came up with during the regressions, but which are all interesting in terms of fleshing out Shakespeare's life as we know it. We start with Shakespeare returning to his old school, enjoying the status of celebrity:

"I can see a big stone building with a square bell tower. It's like a church but I don't think it is. It's long, with three entrances sticking out along the side. It's a college. I go inside through the first entrance. There are long desks and people learning inside. I'm being greeted by a man. The name Harold Wilkins keeps coming to me. I know him. I'm revisiting the place, like I'm an old pupil. I feel I was there as a teenager rather than as a child. I feel I have happy memories of the place - it's somewhere I enjoyed. Two places keep coming to me, Warwick and Gloucester. I'm being introduced to some of the young lads who are about 12-13 years old. I'm about 30 and I feel I've done well for myself. This class is a place of poetry and verse. This teacher Harold Wilkins taught me. I'm talking to the boys, encouraging them. I'm telling them a story, about travelling and the ports I've seen, about the great storm. I have a habit of putting my foot on a stool whilst I'm telling the story. I'm telling the story with a lot of emotion. They're paying attention and enjoying it. I'm putting a lot into it, acting out some of the things I've seen, walking up and down and using my arms and the way I stand and walk to make points. I'm leaving now. I can see rolling hills and a wooded area. I get into a carriage. I feel I'm going to Gloucester."

It has always been assumed that Shakespeare was educated at Kings New School in Stratford upon Avon, though no evidence of this survives. Could it be, however, that the young Shakespeare was not educated there but somewhere else? Or did he (as was usual in grammar school education at that time) move to a higher school in another town when he reached the age of 10 or 11? Terry's feelings of Shakespeare being in his teens whilst at the school as a pupil would suggest this. Was Shakespeare taught not in Stratford but in Gloucester or Warwick? Was he inspired by the teaching of a long-forgotten school master called Harold Wilkins?

There is also a credible tradition that Shakespeare had himself been a school teacher. This was reported by William Beeston, an actor who was the son of Christopher Beeston, a member of Shakespeare's company The Lord Chamberlain's Men. He stated that though Shakespeare 'had but little Latin and less Greek, he understood Latin pretty well: for he had been in his younger years a schoolmaster in the country.' Could it be that Terry was reliving the successful playwright's return to the school at which he had taught?

We cannot tell of course, but if Terry's impressions were imaginary, he would surely have simply recollected going to school in Stratford? This would make sense given his almost non-existent prior knowledge of Shakespeare and his life. To come up with going to school outside Shakespeare's home town is, I feel, unlikely, and I think gives greater credence to the probability of Terry's experiences being real not imagined.

The Gloucester connection came through again in another of Terry's regressions, in which once more Shakespeare appeared to be being feted as a celebrity:

"I'm in Gloucester again, at a reception. It's like a civic reception or a banquet for the guilds, at something like the town hall. I'm in the hall, talking about my travels to an invited audience. There's a

strong maritime connection there, and they're sitting on what look like church pews. There's also a famous traveller being honoured. He's a seafarer. I'm also reading some of my poems and presenting the leaders of the town with a book. It's almost as though I don't know whether I'm there for the poems or the travelling."

Although this was only a short experience for Terry, I find it interesting in that it once more suggests the veracity of his memories. This is because of his reference to Shakespeare making a presentation of a book of poems. In the early years of his career as a writer , Shakespeare published two narrative poems, Venus and Adonis (1593) and The Rape of Lucrece (1594), before his Sonnets were printed in 1609. This is not what the average, non-academic person who knew little about Shakespeare would come up with if they were merely imagining or fantasising scenes from the life of Shakespeare. If Terry was simply making stories up whilst in trance, surely he would have talked exclusively about plays rather than poems?

Another, somewhat curious session found a somewhat humbler Bard standing in awe at the tomb of England's previous greatest writer, before another memory came through in which he was once more the centre of attention:

"I'm in a big, school-type building with lots of small glass panes and ornate brickwork on the outside. It's like a cathedral but I also think it's a place of learning. It's Westminster Abbey. It's dark inside but lit by candles. I'm wearing clothes of brown leather with stripes, and strips of dark red between the stripes. The trousers are like pantaloons. On my head is a soft, brown kid-leather, broad-brimmed hat with a buckle on it. I'm looking at something near the entrance on the right-hand side on the corner, beneath a big stained-glass window. I'm alone there, looking at the tomb of Chaucer. I'm paying my respects to him, I feel as if I have a lot of respect for him."

[Just as an aside, Chaucer was buried in Poet's Corner in Westminster Abbey in 1566-the first writer to be interred there.] Terry was quiet for a while before he moved on:

"I'm in London now, at the theatre to see a play with a load of friends and I'm the centre of attention. I seem to be really well known and I feel full of confidence. I reckon I'm in my mid-thirties. The theatre's horseshoe-shaped with two big support posts on either side of a deep stage. There are boxes or lengths of boxes for seating, which are two high and then one complete horseshoe of seats all the way round. The boxes are sectioned off into seven sections, three on either side and then one in the middle. The place is lit by oil on stanchions. The roof is covered but not completely. The play is one of mine. I can see like a pageant with plenty of people involved. There's no fun in the play, it's heavy, grim. It finishes and the audience is applauding and I'm being congratulated. Now we're walking to a grey stone castle with round turrets. It's not far from the theatre. There are lots of people going back there after the play for a reception. A woman dressed like a queen is there, with a couple of French poodles running around her. She's in her early twenties, wearing a bluey, silver dress and a blue velvet bonnet on her head. She's leading the crowd from the theatre to the castle. I'm sitting next to her and she's just said something like 'you shall be buried amongst them William.' That's something to do with me being at Westminster Abbey. I feel on top of the world, as if I've made it. I'm telling her about The Merchant of Venice. It's written and ready to be performed. She's going to put some money in to back the play, to pay for the costumes. She's going to get the people who make her dresses to make some of the costumes. I feel a lot of warmth and acceptance, as if I'm the star of the show."

We were unsure as to the identity of the aristocratic lady (Terry felt that she might have been a member of royalty) but I think it's not outside the realms of possibility that a wealthy patroness would want to sponsor the costumes in his next production. Once more, Terry appears to have unconsciously got the dates right. He felt he was in his mid-thirties, which would be in the mid-to-late 1590's, the time when Shakespeare wrote his romantic comedies, including The Merchant of Venice. This was also around the time (1599) when Shakespeare and his acting colleagues built and opened the Globe Theatre in Bankside. Could it be that Terry was re-experiencing the opening of the theatre? His description of it does seem very like the design of an Elizabethan playhouse, with its rounded shape (a 'horseshoe' as Terry described it), tiers of galleries, pillars on either side of the stage and an open roof. If this is the case, then Shakespeare would indeed have been in his mid-thirties.

Once more, I question if Terry had been making all this up, what are the chances of him getting so much right?

Chapter 29

The Travelling Thespian

We all know of Shakespeare as one of the greatest writers in the English language and the world's pre-eminent dramatist. However, I think we tend to forget that in his time he was also a jobbing actor, performing with different acting troupes. His name first appears in print in 1594 where he appeared in two productions at the Royal Palace in Greenwich. These performances for Queen Elizabeth I were with an acting company, The Lord Chamberlain's Men, a group of thespians with whom he stayed until he retired from the stage altogether. Although there are few contemporary references to him as an actor, it is reported that he appeared specifically as the Ghost in Hamlet as well as in the works of other fellow dramatists. He is mentioned in Ben Jonson's collected works in 1616 as one of the 'principal comedians'. The First Folio that gathered all his plays together in 1623 (some seven years after his death) puts him at the head of 'the Principal Actors in all these Plays'.

Some of the most fascinating scenes that Terry relived in his regressions brought out elements of Shakespeare the dramatic artist. Remember, I did not guide him or lead him in any way to envisage scenes or themes from Shakespeare's life. Once I had taken Terry into trance I allowed his subconscious mind free rein to take him anywhere into the past life, and the only questions I asked him were open, simple ones such as 'what's happening now?' or 'tell me more about that'. Occasionally I would ask him for specifics such as 'how do you feel?' or 'approximately how old are you?' What came through regarding Shakespeare the performer is intriguing. In one session, Terry relived the excitement of what felt like a modern-day, stand-up comedy routine:

"I'm about 25 or 26 and we're in a small theatre or church-type place. There's not a lot of room in here, but there is a stage. People can sit or stand. It's in a village, I think it's east of Banbury. We're all playing a part and we're making comments to the audience from the stage. One of the actors and me are mixing it with the audience so it's like a three-way thing. His name is John Roe or Roach and he's egging the audience on, getting them involved. He's telling them to give me some stick and I give him and the audience some back. It's getting the audience going and it's during the play, as if it's part of it. It's really fun and a way of keeping the audience involved. They're laughing and responding. I feel like I'm in charge, improvising, inviting comments and enjoying the banter. There's a woman and a man backstage, she's getting things ready for us and he's holding a drum and a stick covered in animal skin. Somebody in the audience is part of the production. He's planted there and is leading the audience. They're having a good time. Somebody's going round with a hat and someone puts an egg in it."

All the way through this Terry had a big smile on his face and a chuckle in his voice. Shakespeare as 'Principal Comedian' indeed.

In another session, whilst in trance, Terry found himself in a horse-drawn coach leaving Gloucester:

"I'm on my way south, back to work. It's the season for plays. It feels warm, maybe May-time. I've got two plays going on at different places. One's near the Tower of London, the other one's south-east along the river, on the other side of the Thames. I'm organising the one in the south-east but I'm acting in the other one - it's where all the important people are. I'm at the theatre near the Tower now, and it absolutely stinks. There's just filth everywhere. It's close, humid, there's no air and the narrow streets are smelly. I wish I was back in the countryside."

Once more Terry was correct. London playgoers did indeed

watch plays during the season (spring and summer), when the less salubrious parts of the city would have been at their worst. The poor were crowded into slum tenements and back alleys, so narrow that the upper storeys blocked out the sunlight. Rubbish was thrown out from windows onto the streets below and urine and excrement ran in the channels. Disease was rife and infestations of rats led to periods of plague. No wonder Shakespeare must have loved and yearned for the clear, open skies of Italy or the English countryside.

I asked him to tell me if he had any other memories of plays being performed. He continued with some vague memories of being in an open-roofed, round theatre watching a play which had some midgets or dwarves in it, before he moved onto to a much clearer scene:

"I'm going across that bridge again in a coach, to the south of the Thames. I feel really busy. There's a church just over the bridge and to the left of the church is a theatre being built with wooden beams and big bricks. It's next to the church and there a plenty of people working on it. I'm involved in it and Charles Worthy is there too. It's like we're working towards an opening or completion date. I'm walking around the outside. I feel really good, like I've a lot to do with why its here. One of the important things is the way the roof is made to let light in. It's a round, high, wooden open roof but it has something like a fringe of overlapped willow on it, intertwined to give more cover against the weather. It juts out, hanging over the edge of the roof. There are main doors going in and wooden seating all around, to left and right. There are spiral steps up to the balcony, and wooden steps down from the stage.
Charles and me are sitting in the front row, watching a rehearsal in the theatre. There are actors dressed as animals in it, one of them dressed as an ass with an ass's head on. It's the first play to be performed there - it's one of mine. I've moved on now to the opening night and there's a fanfare and a procession of people going into the

theatre. They're an invited audience and they've come as a group.
They're all chatting. There are some important people there. It's an
early summer's evening with a blue sky. I can see pennants flick-
ering on the breeze on the outside of the building. I think the play is
Much Ado About Nothing - the title itself has amused the audience.
It's very busy at the back of the stage. I'm not performing, but I
introduce the play. I feel about thirty-something."

Could this be a memory of the building and opening of the Globe
Theatre? This was built by Shakespeare's acting troupe, The Lord
Chamberlain's Men, in 1599. Following a dispute with the
landlord of a playhouse called The Theatre in Shoreditch, the
company pulled The Theatre down under cover of darkness on
the night of the 15th December 1598. They ferried the timber from
the dismantled building across the Thames to Bankside and
constructed the Globe Theatre on the South Bank of the Thames
at Southwark. This was the first playhouse built by actors for
actors and was a more splendid theatre than any London had yet
seen. It was built on garden plots and grounds in the parish of St
Saviour, close to the big church of St Mary Overy. Terry specifically mentioned it being 'next to the church'. Although it is
known that one of the first plays performed there after it opened
in autumn 1599 was Julius Caesar, there is no record of the play
which was performed on its opening night. Terry's impressions
do seem to be confused, as he appears to be alluding to watching
a rehearsal of A Midsummer Night's Dream before he remembered the opening night as Much Ado About Nothing. I cannot
explain this discrepancy, though I suppose it is possible that the
theatre had two opening performances, perhaps one for the
general public (who would have found A Midsummer Night's
Dream to be highly entertaining) and one for the nobility
(including possibly members of royalty or the court) who would
have enjoyed the slightly more sophisticated Much Ado About
Nothing.

Either way, Terry's dates were once more correct, as both plays had been written before the Globe's opening (the earliest printed text states that they were 'sundry times publicly acted' prior to 1600), so they could have been used to open the new theatre. As well as this, Terry again had Shakespeare's age correct ('thirty-something'), as the playwright would have been 35 when the Globe opened for business. Once more, this is surely too much of a coincidence for an unlearned, retired boxing trainer to have got right. I must say that the image of Shakespeare standing on stage introducing his production to a first night London audience is an exciting one.

Chapter 30

The Travelling Troubadour

In further sessions Terry relived memories of Shakespeare the travelling actor and playwright which are not factually known in connection to his life, but which fit very much with what historians know of the period.

He initially found himself again with Charles Worthy, studying a scroll of parchment together:

> "I'm looking at a map of middle England, with scrolling, long hand writing on it. It shows Stratford, Banbury, Oxford and Gloucester. It's something to do with theatre sites. I'm standing outside, in the rolling hills to the west of Oxford and to the east of Gloucester. I can see miles in every direction, seeing rounded hills. I'm with Charles Worthy, the backer, talking about setting up theatres or performances outside of London. He owns a lot of land around here and he's definitely big in Gloucester, something to do with the Merchant's Guild and shipping. He's got power and money and is backing me... Now I'm in a big, ornate hall at a banquet. It's like a guildhall with tradesmen and merchants, and I think it's in Gloucester. It's so ornate it's more like the inside of a church and our voices are echoing. We're talking about money."

Terry paused, before continuing:

> "The next place is Oxford. The same sort of thing but it's not as free and easy, there's no food or drink involved. The people at this meeting are much more serious. We're in a decent sized house with a terrace that backs onto the river. We're talking about bringing the plays out of London, when the season there is over. The plays are

going to be put on in these big houses and not a purpose-built theatre... Next I go to London, on the north side of the river near St Paul's Cathedral. I'm in a small room telling a group of actors where we'll be going. There are three or four midgets amongst them and they're all pleased because it means more work for them."

He then moved onto a later time, when the tour was underway:

"I can see a bloke washing horses, big horses that have been pulling big carriages that are carrying the gear - props and stuff like that. One fellow in the group is called Lucien. We've been travelling country roads, heading for Oxford. It's evening and we're in a small village or town half way between London and Oxford. We're setting up here in order to put a play on. All day has been spent with going into shops and little businesses and inns telling people there's going to be a play on. It might be Windsor. Everyone is standing in a courtyard and a clown is going round taking money off the people, getting them to throw money in a pointed hat. Some of the men actors are dressed as women. I'm reading from a scroll - 'Welcome one, welcome all, to gaze on these actions in their all, you may laugh, you may weep, but please give kindly to help their keep'. The play's funny, with the actors talking to the crowd, who keep reacting. After the performance we're all drinking ale and eating. The actors dressed up as women are absolutely in stitches. We're sitting on big thick, long old benches eating hot pork and bread. I acted in the play - it was one of mine. It must have been funny as the next day when we're travelling on everybody is still laughing about the night before. I feel as if I write a play after this visit to Windsor. We're moving on to Oxford, crossing a stone bridge. When we get there we put another play on. We've got to improvise more because this play has something to do with the Roman military, so I borrow some cloth which is purple and ruby red. We're in a big house getting changed, using the balcony outside as a stage. The audience is on the outside. On the right-hand side of the

balcony is someone reading to the audience, telling them what each scene's about. This is a much more formal job, to an audience of business people. This is the aim of the tour. This is the back of someone's stately home, a big blue-grey house next to the river, to an invited audience. The balcony is paved with steps down to the grass. Because it's stone I can hear the soldiers' footsteps echo as they walk across the stage, metal on brick as they walk up the steps, like a sound effect. It's hot and the play's about 3 hours long. There must be over one hundred people in the audience, all seated. It's hard work, with only about 15 in the company and everyone's got at least two roles to play. Off stage and changing and then back out on stage again. We rest after about an hour, then another hour's work and then another rest. We finish the play but it's been really hard work, and as we head off through the narrow streets everyone's tired. We head west next, to Gloucester, with our carts and horses. When we get there the day is spent walking round Gloucester telling people about the plays. Some of the performers are dressed in costume doing this. It's September/October time, and I think we're there for a while, a good month. We use some of the local people who help out with the acting. It's like there's a theatre base here for the company. We go through an archway or gateway out of the town towards an amphitheatre. It's the site of a Roman amphitheatre on the north-east side of Gloucester where we perform in the open. We get our money by walking round with a bag during the play getting people to put money in it. Some people bring food (I can see bread, milk, beer and rock-hard dark pork). We do several different plays whilst we're here. One of them is done as it's getting dark. There's just a table and two chairs and two actors. There's a lighted candle on the table and some candles behind the actors. The light makes it look really dramatic with lots of shadows. It's a serious play with a long scene with lots of dialogue. It's a king talking to a baron or somebody, discussing a battle. It's very dramatic. The actors go around again for some coin. We finish there and we travel back further south, towards London with a couple of new actors with us. The tour's been a success. We camp out in hilly countryside, putting straw around for the horses. We've got one more place to go, and it's going to take a couple of days before we get to Reading."

An interesting aside here is that when I began researching Terry's memories after we had finished the sessions I looked on the internet for details of a Roman amphitheatre in Gloucester but could find no such structure is known to historians. I wondered if Terry was mistaken and he was remembering Shakespeare's company playing not in an amphitheatre in Gloucester but in some Roman ruins which may still have been standing in the 16th Century. Either that, or he may have got his geography wrong and been appearing in the amphitheatre at nearby Cirencester. However, I spotted a chance entry on Google to an article in the Gloucester and District Archaeological Research Group (GARDARG) Annual Review entitled 'Where was Gloucester's Amphitheatre?' In this paper GARDARG member Nigel Spry writes that it would have been surprising if a major Roman town like Gloucester did not have a substantial amphitheatre at some point in its development (he states that it would have been 'unacceptably humiliating' for Gloucester not to have had one whilst its rival Cirencester did). He points to an area to the south-east of old Roman Gloucester where ancient field boundaries suggest a likely place for such a structure to have been built. Although this is historical conjecture, once more I was impressed by Terry coming up with such a fact that does have a real ring of truth about it.

Our final foray into the life of the travelling troupers proved to be an amusing one, with an alcoholic celebration of cider-time putting paid to any thoughts of public performance. Terry found the company camped for the night near a stream, on the way to Reading:

"It's the next day and we're washing in the stream. There's no food for breakfast and it's going to take most of the day to get there. We take plenty of water with us. When we arrive at Reading there's a fountain, like a spring in the centre of the town with water troughs for horses and it's where people come to collect water. It's not a big place, more of a market town. There's a lot of thatch. It's a farming place, with pigs and geese on the loose. We're going to perform here but also rest. We're in a big, wooden barn with bails of hay at the back and we're going to put a show on in here. I can see big barrels and a press for apples, with massive wooden bars on the top for pressing down."

After a pause Terry smiled as he went on:

"There was going to be a show but everybody's drunk. It's autumn and it's the end of the growing season. It's still not cold and there's a big celebration in the town. There are spits of meat roasting on them and lots of free cider, which people have brought. We just drink and eat. I can smell the meat - pork, and cider, straw and the smell of animals. We all have hangovers in the morning. All we want to do is drink cold water. Nobody's interested in the show so we load up with our gear and cooked meat and cider. The flagons are rounded, bulbous with a wide base. We leave and are on our way again, this time towards Windsor. We go into the castle there to put a play on. Everyone's filthy. We're cleaning ourselves with rags and some water we've been given. The play doesn't need all of us. It's set at one end of a big hall, and the audience are all nobility, courtiers and the like. Verona keeps coming to mind. Somebody explains each scene before it's played, and this seems to shorten the play. We need to keep them interested."

In our sessions together I duly noted down all of the above verbatim as Terry experienced the memories whilst in trance. However, I didn't really pay much attention to the detail, thinking that the idea of Shakespeare being part of a travelling group of actors was a possibility but little else. It was only when I began to research Terry's recollections that I was shocked to find it a real probability. As I mentioned earlier, it is a documented fact that in Elizabethan times companies of performers toured far and wide. It is difficult to say whether Terry was experiencing one of the excursions of Her Majesty's Players (of which he is thought to have been a member) or an unknown tour of The Lord Chamberlain's Men (it is known he was a leading member in 1594).

After the session I asked Terry how old he felt Shakespeare was during the above tour, and he said that he was in his mid-thirties. If Terry's memories were real and the tour around the Midlands actually took place, it seems likely that it would have occurred before the opening of the Globe Theatre in 1599. One can imagine that once The Lord Chamberlain's Men had their own state-of-the-art playhouse in London they would have mainly performed there, rather than undergoing the arduous task of touring with all the difficulties that would entail. Having said that, the outbreak of plague in 1603 closed the London theatres so there is a possibility the tour took place as a result of that, but my guess is that it took place in the years prior to the opening of the Globe.

Once more, though, some of Terry's detail does correspond with what is actually known. His mention of male actors dressed as women is factual as women were not permitted to appear on stage in Elizabethan times. Female parts in plays were taken by male actors. Also, Terry mentioned Verona at the end of the outdoor performance in Windsor, which could be a reference to Shakespeare's play The Two Gentlemen of Verona. If the tour he described did take place in the 1590's, this would fit as this play is known to be one of the Bard's early Italianate comedies. Similarly, Terry said that after the performance in Windsor he felt that he wrote a play, almost it seems as a response to being there.

If this was so, could this have been The Merry Wives of Windsor? This too would fit as it is thought the play was written prior to 1597 (it was first published in 1602). Although not academic Terry was certainly not stupid and like most of us during his life would have heard the titles of Shakespeare's plays without knowing the content. If he was making all this up, the chances are he would have given me names of late, well-known plays which were not yet written during this earlier period of Shakespeare's life, which did not happen at any time in our sessions together. In my opinion, details like this make it more likely that Terry truly was the reincarnation of Shakespeare.

Chapter 31

Shakespeare's Women, and a Mystery Man

Very little is known about Shakespeare's marriage to Anne Hathaway. They married in 1582 when he was 18 and she is thought to have been 28 years old. Six months later Anne gave birth to a daughter and twins two years later. In his will he left the bulk of his estate to his eldest daughter Susanna but the will itself contains barely a mention of his wife Anne. He did make a point, however, of leaving her 'my second best bed', a bequest that has led to a great deal of speculation. Some scholars see this as being an insult to Anne, whereas others believe that the second best bed denotes the matrimonial bed and therefore rich in significance.

It has to be said though, that one must wonder just how close their marriage must have been once Shakespeare became a travelling player or moved to London to become a successful playwright. The likelihood is that Anne remained in Stratford to bring up the children whilst William forged a career in the capital. If this was the case, then this may have suited Shakespeare as a convenient arrangement, allowing him to enjoy romantic dalliances with other women (and how much opportunity he must have had as a leading actor and playwright in London). When they married she was probably seven or eight years older than her husband, and at 26 perhaps a bit long in the tooth in terms of the marriage stakes. She became pregnant to a teenaged lover and then married him. Did Shakespeare reluctantly submit to this, and then lead a livelier life than we think? Certainly, some of his Sonnets (written to 'a Dark Lady') would suggest this.

In Terry's regressions we touched upon Anne Hathaway only

fleetingly, but what was more interesting to me was Terry's memories of an unrecorded love affair. This is obviously unknown to historians, but I wonder if Terry has stumbled upon something which brings the somewhat dry, factual knowledge of Shakespeare some passion and depth. During a session Terry reported that a woman kept coming in to his mind, together with the name Bridget. I asked him to allow himself to move towards any memories that connected with this. After a few seconds of silence he responded:

"I get a strong sense that she's from Banbury and that she's his mistress. I'm with her, outside her cottage. It's a small place. She's about 25. She's just said 'don't go back there'. The name Bridget Farnon keeps coming to me. We're hugging. She's not rich. She might even be a servant or something, dressed in a frock and a pinafore and a white-fringed, soft hat. I get a feeling of tension coming from Anne, who I feel is a bossy woman who creates tension, whilst Bridget's a nice lass. Anne, I think, is really bossy. I've been staying here, relaxing, and it feels really good but her parents are not happy. They live in the house too. She's younger than me. I'm sure this is in Banbury. We have to finish the relationship as her parents are not approving. They're arguing that it's not good for their daughter. There is an age difference but that's not the main problem - they think it's ruining her chances. I feel really sad as I leave and I head back to Stratford. I go home and put some clothes together. I'm going to London for a while. I go to the big house across the river where I went originally to show the backer the work. It's a different situation now though, as I've got my own room there and the run of the house and servants doing for me. I feel I'm about 38 and things are really happening for me. Anne just thinks I'm in London working, but I'm sad, trying to get over Bridget. I'm very busy, with plays and something going on every night. Anne comes down to stay and she's amazed at how popular the plays are and the lifestyle I'm leading. We're in a hall in a big house, a Duke's place or something.

There are invites to banquets all over the place. It's as if everybody
wants to meet me but it's too much for Anne, she just wants to get
home."

Terry paused, as if experiencing a passage of time, before he
continued:

"I think there must be a season for plays, maybe finishing in
October. I'm on my way home, travelling straight up to Stratford.
I'm going to miss Banbury. There are leaves coming down every-
where." He sighed sadly. *"I'm walking with Anne. I just keep*
saying 'what am I going to do with all this fame and fortune?' She
doesn't want to do any travelling and I think I'm going to cut my
travelling down. I feel I've done enough. I feel that we're going to
spend more time together. I'm in Stratford and a lot of old friends
are greeting me. I'm strolling around, reminiscing and reflecting. I
feel as if I'm slowing down in myself. It's cold and I go back home
and sit in front of the fire with a warm drink of hock. It tastes
soothing."

It seems that Shakespeare resigns himself to a life at home with
Anne. If he was 38 when this love affair with Bridget ended he
had approximately 14 years of his life left, and Terry felt that he
starts to slow down and live a more settled life. It is accepted that
from his 42nd year onwards Shakespeare wrote fewer plays and
there is a tradition that he retired to Stratford some years before
his death. Again, Terry's memories confirm what is historically
known.

In our last regression session, Terry surprised me by
providing a tantalising glimpse of another suspected side of
Shakespeare's sexuality. He had mentioned to me after an earlier
regression that he had a feeling that Shakespeare, as he put it,
'swings both ways'. I did not respond to this but remembered
that many had questioned whether Shakespeare had homosexual

tendencies; pointing to several of the sonnets as evidence of his love for a young man (others have read the same passages as the expression of intense friendship rather than sexual love). Some scholars have highlighted what they see as sub-texts of ambiguous sexuality in some of the plays. For example, Douglas E Green in an essay on A Midsummer Night's Dream explores its 'homoerotic significations.' Either way, Terry's memories suggest some deep feelings for another man:

> *"It's daytime and I'm sitting, leaning against a fallen tree-trunk under another tree, by a cottage. I feel really good, I'm laughing. There's water not far away, a winding stream, and it's very green. A few miles to the west in open countryside is a big country house, a light-grey building with lots of windows and glass. I'm in England and I feel about 25-26. There's a man dressed as a woman – that's why I'm laughing. He's in a big frilly dress. The cottage is not home, but a place I come to relax...I've moved to a later time, maybe aged 38, and I can feel a strong emotion with the man now. It represents freedom to me."*

At this point Terry began to breathe heavily, his face flushed and betraying signs of emotion. His hands were tense. I had seen him like this before in our sessions, when he would do his best to keep a stiff upper lip and not show how emotional he felt.

> *"It's a very happy time. We're near Banbury and his name's Ben, and he's quite flamboyant. He has a straight, thin nose, a large forehead and thin eyes, and a small goatee-type beard. There's a real friendship as well as romance, we were friends long before either of us knew we had feelings for each other. I have a feeling of relief and freedom."*

After all of the emotion Terry began to compose himself and, frustratingly, came out of trance, signalling that he wanted to finish at that point. Could the mystery lover have been Ben Jonson, Shakespeare's great friend and rival? Later on I showed Terry a picture of Jonson and he thought that he was not the Ben in his memory, but I'm not so sure.

History has it that Shakespeare and Jonson were good friends, with their first documented contact taking place in 1598 when Shakespeare acted in Jonson's new play 'Every Man In His Humour'. This was one of Jonson's early successes before he became an established playwright. One early legend has it that Shakespeare recommended the play to his acting troupe the Lord Chamberlain's Men, thus ensuring its success. It is also said that after this he recommended Jonson's writings to the public.

Further traditions have Jonson and Shakespeare drinking together and of Shakespeare being the godfather of one of Jonson's children. It was even said that Shakespeare contracted his fatal 'ague' because of a 'merry meeting' with Jonson and another poet in Stratford.

More tellingly, perhaps, is Jonson's own comment in his 'Discoveries' that he 'loved the man'. Were these words more significant than literary history has given credence to? Was Jonson dropping a big hint as to the reality of their relationship? Ben Jonson would fit in with Terry's description of having known this mystery lover for some time as a friend before the relationship became a romance, as the records show that the two writers had known each other for a number of years before Shakespeare's death.

Regardless of the true identity of 'Ben' as remembered by Terry, could it be that he had remembered something which is suspected but factually unknown to historians? I realise that for many people the idea of the Bard of Avon being bisexual may be heresy, but I can only report exactly what Terry experienced when in trance. What is interesting to me, as I've said earlier on in this section of the book on Shakespeare, is that if Terry was making all of these memories up, I would not at any time have expected him to have fabricated memories of Shakespeare being bi-sexual. I doubt very much that he would have had any knowledge of the suspicions, harboured by some literary historians that the Sonnets suggest as much. As well as this, Terry's emotional state when he experienced the meeting with 'Ben' was unusual, in that he tended not to give vent to his feelings when in trance. For him to visibly show the depth of his emotions suggest to me the truth of his memories.

Chapter 32

The Death of Shakespeare

In my final session with Terry I asked him to experience the time of Shakespeare's death. Factually, nothing is known as to the cause of the 52-year-old's death on 23rd April 1616. He was buried in Holy Trinity Church, Stratford upon Avon two days later. Terry's re-experiencing of this was a little hazy, but this could have been because he was experiencing Shakespeare's physical symptoms as he expired:

"I'm travelling up from London to Stratford, just passing through Banbury. I'm not on a coach, just a little wagon. I feel I'm well known by the travelling merchants. It's a slow journey, with lots of little villages. I feel I've left London because I feel terrible, I feel really ill. My face and hands are white."

Terry's breathing was slow and laboured, and he spoke softly and hoarsely. After a long pause, he continued in a low voice:

"I'm on the outskirts of a village. I can see a church with a square bell tower but no steeple. The name St Giles comes to mind. I can see a white cottage and a river winds around the back of the house. There's a stream running into the river from the back of the house. The church is on the other side of a bridge, on the left. The cottage is set in greenery and I can see a hill and a big tree at the top. Something's happened here. The top half of my lip and part of my side has gone numb. I wonder if I'm having a stroke. It feels as if I believe I can move on, but I'm laid with my back to this cottage, looking at the water in front of it. I'm having a stroke here, but it's not frightening. The sun's in the sky on my right, so it's going to

set behind me. I'm alone and the sun is going round behind me and I can't move. I'm just laid here. I can feel numbness in my body, like a coolness, and I can't move. A woman finds me. She can't move me so she goes to get help. A miller comes with his horse and cart, wearing a hood. He lays me inside the cottage on a wooden bed. There's no canopy over it, just the bed. I can't say or do anything. I see the flickering flame of the fire. It's a big, wide, brick fireplace. The left side of my body feels cold, and the cold is spreading to my toes and fingers and now to the other side of my body. The woman has dark hair, aged about 40-ish. She keeps slinging logs on the fire but it's not making any difference. She's watching over me and crying, but there's nothing I can say. I know I'm dying. I'm thinking about Bridget Farnon. Things are going white."

Terry heaved a big sigh and was silent for a time. I asked him how he felt. All he said was *"peaceful"*. The end had come. The Swan of Avon was no more.

Could it be that Shakespeare died in or near to Banbury, having had a stroke there? Shakespeare had executed his last will and testament in March 1616 so there is a possibility that he was already feeling unwell. From Terry's description it seems that he was travelling home to Stratford when he suffered the fatal stroke in the Banbury area. This does make sense as it is thought that Shakespeare continued travelling to London from Stratford in his later years, having retired from the stage. It is known that in 1614 he was in London with his son-in-law. It's interesting that Terry's last thoughts as Shakespeare died were of Bridget, the woman who he loved but with whom he was not allowed to spend his life.

Thus ended, for Terry and me, our explorations into the hidden life of Shakespeare. So much of what he'd experienced fitted in with what is known by historians, and I feel his memories add a great deal to our understanding of England's greatest literary genius. I feel that we got a real sense of

Shakespeare the human being, a man of creative energy, of passion and wit, a man with a love of travel, a love of love, and a love of life itself. All this from Terry, a truly genuine and honest man, who had never read anything about Shakespeare in his life. Do I think he is the reincarnation of Shakespeare? Of course I do. I sincerely hope that Terry's story, as well as those of my other clients featured in this book, will give you pause for thought as you consider the concept of reincarnation in your own life. If it helps you to be curious about your own past lives, then so much the better.

POSTSCRIPT

As with the other 'main players' in this book, I asked Terry to write a few words giving his thoughts on the therapy process he had experienced with me. It feels apt that his words should close his extraordinary story:

Before I met Steve I had been suffering from depression, anxiety and a feeling of worthlessness, all due to stress at work and other issues. I had visited my GP but found it really difficult to explain my problems to him. I am a 'bloke', supposed to be strong mentally and physically. I am also a very private person who prefers to work my way through problems rather than ask for help from anyone, but I needed to speak to someone confidentially. I was offered prescription drugs but refused them. Around this time I had an Italian exam coming up and this led me to Steve. I had heard him on the radio and wondered if he could clear the constant fuzz and fog in my head. I was glad we met. In the initial session he taught me relaxation techniques and subsequent sessions led to Past Life Regression and a long fantastic journey. I can best describe how I felt during our sessions as entering a part of the past life at one particular time. For instance, each time I regressed the same pattern followed: I entered through a door into another time in the past and a series of events took place in the past life. I could not force a memory, nor could I expand on any details except the ones that were laid out before me. Once the memories had been relived that was it, it was akin to clearing out the garage and once it was over everything was neat and tidy and in its place. I did go through the full gamut of emotions but I always came out of trance completely relaxed and refreshed. Steve has asked if he can write this story in his book and I have said yes just as long as I can retain my anonymity, as I explained earlier I am a very private person. But believe me these things happened. He also solved my problems and I still practice the relaxation techniques he taught me. I owe him big time.

THE END

BOOKS

O is a symbol of the world, of oneness and unity. In different
cultures it also means the "eye," symbolizing knowledge and
insight. We aim to publish books that are accessible, constructive
and that challenge accepted opinion, both that of academia and
the "moral majority."

Our books are available in all good English language
bookstores worldwide. If you don't see the book on the shelves
ask the bookstore to order it for you, quoting the ISBN number
and title. Alternatively you can order online (all major online
retail sites carry our titles) or contact the distributor in the
relevant country, listed on the copyright page.

See our website **www.o-books.net** for a full list of over 500
titles, growing by 100 a year.

And tune in to myspiritradio.com for our book review radio show,
hosted by June-Elleni Laine, where you can listen to the authors
discussing their books.

9781846944949